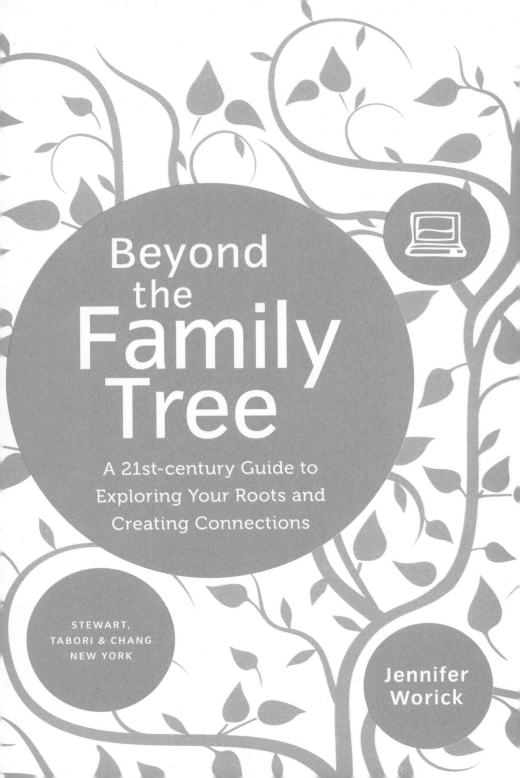

Beyond the Family Tree

A 21st-century Guide to
Exploring Your Roots and
Creating Connections

STEWART,
TABORI & CHANG
NEW YORK

Jennifer
Worick

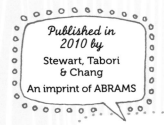

Published in 2010 by
Stewart, Tabori & Chang
An imprint of ABRAMS

Editor:
Dervla Kelly

Designer:
LeAnna Weller Smith

Production Manager:
Tina Cameron

Text copyright © 2010 by Jennifer Worick

Interior photographs copyright © 2010 by Jennifer Worick

Author photograph copyright © 2010 by Nicholas Utke

The text of this book was composed in **CongressSans**, *Monoline Script*, and **Museo**.

Printed and bound in the United States of America
10 9 8 7 6 5 4 3 2 1

Library of Congress Cataloging-in-Publication Data

Worick, Jennifer.
Beyond the family tree : a 21st-century guide to exploring your roots and creating connections / Jennifer Worick.
p. cm.
Includes bibliographical references and index.
ISBN 978-1-58479-797-5 (alk. paper)
1. Genealogy. I. Title.
CS16.W67 2010
929'.1072—dc22

2009053909

Stewart, Tabori & Chang books are available at special discounts when purchased in quantity for premiums and promotions as well as fundraising or educational use. Special editions can also be created to specification. For details, contact specialsales@abramsbooks.com or the address below.

ABRAMS
THE ART OF BOOKS SINCE 1949

115 West 18th Street
New York, NY 10011
www.abramsbooks.com

To the Woricks, Hamlins, Yechs, Eckelbargers, Miltzes, Steinbachers, and the rest of the family who made this book possible and who have such darn good stories to share.

Table of Contents

Acknowledgments

This book was a true labor of love, coming out of my own desire to connect with my family on a more meaningful and wide-ranging level.

I have to thank my kin for a lot of things—for my good genes, the Cowboy Cookie recipe, my sense of humor, a passel of memories. But I also want to thank them for their generous participation in the creation of *Beyond the Family Tree*. My dad, Willis Worick, shared a treasure trove of childhood photos, and the rest of my family—including mom Judy Eckelbarger, stepmom Pat Worick, stepdad Jim Eckelbarger, brothers Chris and John Worick, and all of my extended family (the Woricks, Hamlins, Yechs, Eckelbargers, and so on)—has supported me throughout the years and throughout this book's publication. I couldn't have done it without them . . . and I wouldn't have wanted to.

I must give props to my amazing agent, Joy Tutela of David Black Agency, for her unwavering support of me, both professionally and personally. Life coach Elizabeth C. Hechtman has also helped me to grow and develop my creative and professional vision through our wide-ranging work over the years.

Beyond the Family Tree would not have happened without my editor, Dervla Kelly, who believed in the book from day one. The rest of the team at STC—including designer LeAnna Weller Smith and copyeditor Karen Fraley—brought their many talents to the table to produce a stylish, solid book that's both fun and informative to read.

Aside from my family, I get by with a lot of help from my friends. In addition to taking my fabulous author photo, Nicholas Utke helped to research equipment and online resources, providing welcome manuscript suggestions along the way. The lovely Rebecca Stevenson shared her insight about effective interviewing techniques, while Ray Medved and Aron Thompson weighed in on the technical aspects of capturing a compelling interview. Thanks also to Sacha Adorno, Jessica Campbell, Kerry Colburn, Michelle Goodman, Jane Hodges, Darcey Howard, Amy Levine, Diane Mapes, Michaela Murphy, Kim Pavlak, Laurel Rivers, Alison Rooney, Kathy Schultz, Stacya Silverman, Rob Sorensen, and Sandra Watson. Their ongoing friendships encourage, educate, and inspire me pretty much every day.

A Book on How to Talk with Your Family? *Seriously?*

Yep. Some of us are fortunate to have great relationships with our immediate and extended family. Others are separated by distance or differences. Regardless of where you fall on the functional family scale, there is always more to learn about each other. *Beyond the Family Tree* will be your handbook on how to forge better family relationships by getting into more interesting conversations and creating an online means of communication.

When I was writing a book on prairie skills, I needed to find out how to milk a cow. I e-mailed my dad, asking if our relatives up north had a dairy farm because I wanted to talk to someone in the know. His wry response? "Uh, I grew up on a farm with cows."

Ouch. After getting over the embarrassment of not thinking about my dad as a cow-milking expert, I started wondering about all the other things I didn't know about him. I began asking him questions about his childhood, what it was like growing up on a farm in rural

Michigan in the 1940s and 50s. What he shared with me was so rich, I wanted more.

What started as a mission with my family turned into *Beyond the Family Tree*. This book is chock-full of conversation starters, questions to help you to create a dialogue during family gatherings or one-on-one get-togethers. But I take it one step further than just a simple book of questions. This is a complete handbook for choosing the right equipment and then—after you've captured meaningful interviews—targeting and using a social media network to stay connected. Sharing content online will allow you to create a living history and provide a place where a current, vibrant dialogue can occur and be sustained.

For instance, I could post this childhood photo of my dad with a puppy.

Cute, huh? It's particularly sweet to me because my dad still has the same impish grin. But the sad thing about this picture and a bunch of other deckle-edged photos of my dad is that I discovered them only a couple of years ago. I've gone decades without seeing these key links to my family history. I'm trying to make up for it now. Posting the photo online allows other family members to witness the cuteness of my dad and his dog. When I posted this online, I asked for comments on the photo but I also invited other family members to talk about and upload photos of *their* favorite pet. We had a beloved dog named Tippy when we were kids, but my brothers now talk about one or several of the pets they've owned as adults with their families. Just posting one simple photo can open up several lines of communication.

Dad

But let's not forget about video. Video footage of family members can be one of the most compelling and fascinating elements to share with one another. For instance, I was home for the holidays a couple of years ago with a video camera and I started asking my parents and siblings about their interests and key moments. They were initially shy in front of the camera, but with a bit of prompting, they opened up and generously shared their opinions and memories. I sometimes got short, not very exciting answers, but by and large, I was thrilled with the wonderful stories that I had never heard before . . . because I never asked.

So how do you *get the goods* from your family? Well, I have a plan. Chapter 1 supplies you with all the tools you'll need to become a capable A/V technician. These days, it's easy to use camcorders and transfer the information to your computer. Many computers come equipped with video editing software so you can clean up your footage and upload it to the Web.

You'll learn how to capture compelling interviews and post video clips from those conversations.

Once you've got your technology figured out, you can turn your attention to conducting the interview. Don't assume that you'll be able to turn the camera on and just go. Chapter 2 will train you how to be an investigative but sensitive reporter. Compelling or revealing conversations can occasionally happen organically but don't count on it. Do your homework. Use the interview advice in this chapter to render your relative comfortable and communicative. Tips on drawing out a person will be covered, so you can get great stories while remaining targeted.

Chapter 3 suggests 1,000 questions to spark a fresh and revelatory dialogue. You will be armed with every line of query imaginable and your conversations with your family will become deeper and more meaningful. I guarantee that by asking a sampling of these questions (conveniently organized by subject) you'll come away with a new appreciation and understanding of any relative.

Once you've gathered great video, audio, or written information, what do you do with it? Chapter 4 will show you how to effectively *use social networks* for family communication. Sure, there's Facebook, YouTube, and Twitter, but how can you use these popular sites—as well as other Web-based resources—specifically for family communications? There are many options available (with more cropping up daily) and I'll help you sort out which online vehicles are the most practical for your purposes. Don't be scared; many of these sites and services are free and easy to navigate.

Throughout this book, you and your family will acquire tools to create a history far beyond scrapbooks and family trees. Not only can you amass a record of memorable events, anecdotes, recipes, and philosophies, you can build better, more dynamic relationships with one another. A special appendix supplies you with worksheets for interview notes and spreadsheets so you can keep track of which family members you've connected with, and which relatives you still need to track down.

After reviewing the ins and outs of your equipment and delving into the art of the interview, you'll be confident and ready to initiate some lively conversations. With the preparation under your belt, rest easy and focus on what's important: your family. There are a lot of conversations to be had, so let's get to it.

chapter 1

Nuts *and* Bolts

You're probably champing at the bit to get to talkin' with your kin. That's understandable—they have a lot to say and time together is precious. Before you head out to Grandma's house, however, take a moment to prep for your conversation. You can still sit around the kitchen table and shoot the breeze, but come armed with a plan. Bring along a camcorder or tape recorder. Think about lighting and audio. Bring a laptop or notebook if you don't have a recording device. Create an outline for your interview. If you have done your homework, you'll be able to relax a bit, which will make for a better interview and overall experience for everyone involved.

I'm no tech wizard. But as I've delved into interviewing family members, I've learned on the job. And I'm not too proud to beg. There are a lot of savvy, generous people out there who know how to capture unbelievable video, can draw out amazing stories and compelling interviews, and are willing to share their expertise. Fortunately, I got them to give up some trade secrets.

I don't want to assume that everyone has the same access to equipment, or that you want to work in only one medium. So I'll start with camcorders and work my way through to good old-fashioned pen and paper, detailing the pros and cons of each method.

There are all sorts of ways to capture a conversation. The important thing is to *have* the talk; how you record it is up to you. Some methods just won't work in various situations. For instance, turning a camera on a parent in the middle of a noisy gathering might prove useless when you look at the footage later. In this case, you're probably better off using a laptop or notebook to capture their comments. This is where planning is crucial. If you know you are going into a less-than-optimal situation, case the joint and create a situation that works for you. In the family gathering scenario, for instance, bring along a tripod and external mic, and set up a guest bedroom or the patio as your "set." Your footage will be much, much better, as will your interview. Your relative will be able to focus on your questions, rather than be distracted by a little one's antics or the spinach dip.

TECH TALK

While it's great to plan *what* you want to ask your family, it's also necessary to map out *how* to do it.

In other words, you need to channel your inner A/V geek and gather some equipment that's going to be effective, reliable, and easy to use. You want to pick the kind of equipment and recording method that will best suit your purposes, not to mention your budget. Peruse your options before making a choice. You might want to use several different methods, depending on your subject matter, your relatives, or your surroundings; be flexible.

To stay within your means, I recommend *setting a budget* for your equipment. Video recorders can cost as little as a couple hundred bucks and as much as, well, a lot. Consider what you and perhaps other contributing members of your family can afford to spend on equipment and then draw up a list of things you need (such as a camera, cassette tapes for storage, or external microphone), as well as a wish list of things you can pick up at a later date (good lighting equipment, computer software, etc.). Work with what you've got and within your means, or the project could become too loaded. What I mean is this: if you invest in a thousand dollars worth of equipment, you're going to feel obligated to produce *Citizen Kane*–worthy video footage.

Beyond the Family Tree

While it might motivate you to keep going with the project, it could also become an albatross hanging around your already anxious neck. That said, let's review basic equipment so you can better assess what will work for your time, budget, and family.

Interviewing Tools

Before you start talking up your family, it's good to get the right gear in place.

✓ *Camcorder* (handheld digital, DVD, hard-drive, or videotape camera recorders)

PROS:

· Captures visual and audio images: *mannerisms, expressions, appearances, inflections, dialect, etc.*
· Portable
· Easy to operate
· Can edit footage and upload to Web
· If set up properly, frees up interviewer to converse with subject and avoid distraction

CONS:

· Requires a quiet place for the interview (ideally)
· Will initially cost a few hundred dollars
· Interview subject may not be comfortable on camera
· Battery can drain after a limited period of time
· Will require some post-production work on the computer

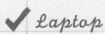 **Laptop**

PROS:
- With a webcam, can record a conversation from an off-site location
- Inexpensive to set up if you already have a laptop
- Dialogue can be typed as the interviewee talks
- Less intimidating than a camcorder

CONS:
- Hard to focus on transcribing an interview while you're conducting it
- You can miss great quotes or stories if you're a poor typist
- Can be tricky or limited when recording with a webcam
- If using a webcam, interviewee has to sit in front of computer and may have hard time looking into webcam
- Can't always control surroundings
- If in different locations, both you and relative need to have a webcam installed and know how to operate it

 Audio recorders (both digital and tape recorders)

PROS:
- Possibly less intimidating than a camcorder
- Inexpensive (for a mini-tape recorder)
- Portable
- Perfect for podcasting

PROS *(continued)*:

· Some digital recorders allow easy sound file uploads
  to your computer

CONS:

· Only captures audio

· Some have confusing function buttons; potential
  for unintentional erasure

· Will require some post-production work on the computer

✓ *Pen and paper*

PROS:

· Cheap

· Very portable

· No learning curve

· Reliable

CONS:

· No audio or video

· Time consuming: must transcribe to upload to a site

· Hand may cramp as you write

· Hard to keep up with the interview unless you know
  shorthand or are really fast, and you will most likely miss
  details or quotes verbatim

· Miss facial expressions and intonations

⇨ Camcorders

Like your family, camcorders come in all shapes and sizes. These portable video recorders may come with a hard drive or use mini-cassettes, DVDs or old-school videotape. There is a *huge* range of equipment available, and there's a video camera for pretty much every budget. You can get a really functional workhorse camcorder for a few hundred bucks.

Even professionals are using small camcorders but often choose a high-definition option if they can afford it (you can pick up a Sony Handycam HD camcorder for around $1,000), as the quality can be phenomenal. But any camcorder can produce very good, usable video. I'd recommend purchasing a camcorder that allows you to record on mini-cassettes or CDs so you have a backup and can build an archive. Never record over your mini-cassettes, as the quality will be diminished. Just label your tapes promptly and store them in a cool, dry, dark place (such as a closet) away from anything that could magnetize them. Choosing between mini-cassettes and CDs is up to you: the backup method is a matter of preference; just check that the camcorder's software is compatible with your computer.

If you want to carry something so you are always ready to capture priceless footage, consider

Beyond the Family Tree

getting a Flip video camcorder. It is small, is available in high-definition, uses AA batteries, and costs between $150 and $200. You can purchase a tripod for it for less than twenty bucks and set up shop in short order with surprisingly good quality. Its small size is nice for portability, but its compact shape will also prove useful during your interview. Soon your relative will become comfortable sitting in front of the Flip camera; he will almost forget it's there. In contrast, larger camcorders make folks acutely aware that they are being filmed and they may become shy or self-conscious, at least initially. In addition, like many camcorders, Flip cameras come with built-in editing software and a built-in USB port, making uploading and sharing video a breeze. You don't have to lug extra cords around; just pull out the port and plug it directly into your computer. It's worth giving this a try if you are getting under way with video; you might find it really handy to keep in your bag. You never know when your aunt is going to bust out with a great anecdote or your goddaughter will give an impromptu dance recital. Be prepared.

When shopping for a camcorder, take into consideration these features:

AUDIO: Look for a camera that has the ability to attach an external audio source, which you might find necessary for noisy spaces or soft-spoken family members. (And just like a mini-cassette, external audio becomes a backup in the event of poor camera audio.)

TRIPOD: Camcorders all allow you to attach a tripod for stability. Trust me, you'll want one. Set it up properly and leave it alone. You can then focus your attention on your relative, not the camera.

SCREEN: Many camcorders feature large screens that swivel, which is convenient if you are interviewing yourself.

MEMORY: Most cameras have built-in memory but this is limited (you might get two hours of footage before you run out of memory). If you are recording several people in a row or your grandfather is going on and on, you could use up all of your camera's memory. Get additional memory cards if you choose a camera without mini-cassettes. If your camera does take cassettes, make sure you have an ample supply on hand if you are doing a marathon recording session; for instance, when all the family is together at the holidays.

RECORDING TIME: Look for a camera with a rechargeable battery that will give you a couple of hours of recording time and that will warn you onscreen when your battery is getting low. This usually coincides with replacing your 60-minute mini-cassette or CD. If you're near a power outlet, keep the camera plugged in during your interview. (Most cameras come with a power adapter as well as an A/V and USB cable that will allow you to watch your interview through a computer, TV, or DVD player.)

RESOLUTION/ZOOM: There are high-definition camcorders on the market but normal ones have surprisingly good resolution and zoom. Since you'll be in close proximity to your relative during the interview, you'll want to zoom only occasionally to capture facial expressions during a particularly rich moment. A camera with 40x optical zoom or 2000x digital zoom is probably not necessary unless you are fascinated with your brother's pores.

STORAGE: If you don't have memory allocated on a hard drive to immediately download your footage from your camcorder's built-in memory, you may want a camcorder that will record your interviews on mini DV cassettes or mini DVD/DVR disks. Label and store the unedited footage after you've transferred the data to your computer and edited the interviews down to manageable bits.

The best thing to do is to make a list of the features most important to you in a camcorder, research various cameras, and then check them out in person at an electronics store before settling on the one that suits your needs and budget. Once you bring one home, perform a few test runs to check out lighting, audio, and staging, as well as to get comfortable with the camcorder's basic operations.

Computer Software

Having the camera is only half the creative battle; you will need something to edit your recorded footage into smaller clips and save it in a format that can be uploaded onto the Internet. Your camcorder might come with software that will allow you to organize your video files, burn them to DVDs, and upload them to the Web. However, the software may be inadequate if you want to do anything beyond basic editing (special intros and exits, graphics, music, text laid over video, etc.).

Computers often come equipped with video editing software. When I first started out recording my family, I used iMovie. I was a complete and utter newbie using this, which is to say I had a steep learning curve over the course of a few days. But I sort of intuited my way around the software until I figured out basic operating procedure. With large files and a laptop that's memory-challenged, I quickly learned to store all of my footage on an external hard drive and work on the files from there. I broke the files into smaller vignettes, starting and stopping at the perfect second. I was also able to add simple graphics to indicate who was speaking or to provide some context as to what was being discussed, where the interview was taking place, and that sort of thing. I resisted the urge to add bells and whistles, such as wild transitions that resembled something out of an 80s New Wave music video. I wanted the focus to be on the person being interviewed; anything other than the simplest of effects distracted from the main event.

Laptop or PDA

Personal Digital Assistants (PDAs) now have some audio recording abilities, and if you're dexterous, you can type some brief notes into your device. But you really need a laptop for on-site interviews and a laptop or desktop computer for editing footage or properly transcribing interviews and uploading them to the Web. Make sure you have a reliable browser and a strong Internet connection when uploading your content; there's nothing more aggravating than spending hours trying to post a video or another file to a site. Technology should make life easier, not create more layers of complication.

⟱ Webcams

Webcams are cameras that are built in or connect to your computer and allow you to record yourself or someone else in the range of its viewfinder. The nice thing is that you can see yourself on-screen so you can adjust your position or the camera for the best composition. Consider setting up a webcam and sitting your relative down in front of the computer. Sit on the other side of the screen out of the frame and ask questions. This would work particularly well if someone has a nice anecdote to share where a static camera shot would work. The audio isn't stellar with a webcam but in the absence of camera equipment, this can prove to be a stopgap solution.

⟱ Audio Recorders

People have long enjoyed audio recordings (both digital and tape recorders) in many forms—phonographs, records, radio, 8-tracks, cassette tapes, CDs, mp3s—and now it's easier than ever to capture sounds and voices.

While video is all the rage and has obvious appeal, don't overlook the *power of audio*. Compelling interviews are constantly turning up in podcasts. Consider your family members. Do any of them have musical abilities? A wonderful, rich voice? A tinkling laugh that is legend? If a relative's voice is notable or if they can dramatically tell a story through sound, don't hesitate to use an audio recorder. You might have an old-school tape

recorder lurking around, but you can also pick up a recording device for a modest price. A friend of mine who creates a crafty podcast loves her Zoom H2 Portable Stereo Recorder. I sort of forgot about audio until I witnessed this rad device. It's a bit spendy (about $150) but it records hours of audio on just a couple of AA batteries, has built-in storage, copies files to a computer easily, features mics on either end so you can record a conversation nicely, and produces decent sound quality (although quieter environments are always preferable to noisy cavernous spaces).

There are cheaper handheld digital recorders as well. The sound quality might not be as pristine and the memory capability not as extensive but for your purposes, a less-expensive recorder might work just fine for recording interviews. There are recorders that use mini-cassettes, which are nice for a backup system. However, if you plan on uploading the audio directly to your computer, you can create an archive on your hard drive rather than having external storage devices. Assess your preferences and existing equipment and then make a list of your most important features; take it with you when shopping for an audio recorder. Whatever you choose, play with the equipment before you sit down for a real interview. You want to be intimately familiar with your device and its capabilities so you can optimize the interview experience for you as well as your family.

Pen and Paper

You don't need expensive high-tech equipment to flesh out great stories from your family. In the "old" days (i.e., before the mid-80s), reporters and the rest of us had to actually take notes by hand until our fingers cramped. So we got pretty good at scribbling down our own secret shorthand or zeroing in on the salient comments and editing out the fat as we went.

You can probably figure this out yourself, but if you intend to take old-school notes, plan ahead. Consider printing out interview forms (see the appendix, page 176) to record your notes or buy a large notebook that will be a pleasure to write in and will contain enough pages to capture all of your family's stories. Consider buying a lovely hardcover book that can serve as a sort of heirloom in progress.

Have several of your favorite pens or pencils on hand. Running out of ink when a story is just getting good is not how you want the scenario to play out. Like a Boy Scout, be prepared.

While paper and pen is a viable way to document an interview or conversation, it *is* limited. To really connect with your family and share your interviews, you will need *some* equipment. While you could photocopy notes for your annual holiday letter, you're constrained unless you transfer your interviews to a digital form. You can then upload the information to a site or account, or share through group e-mails.

PREPARING YOUR "SET"

Before your relative settles into his easy chair or sits down at the kitchen table for an interview, take the time to create a set that will be comfortable and will view well on camera.

Like most things in life, *prepa-ration is key.* Don't take anything for granted. Carefully arrange your set, taking into consideration location, lighting, audio, composition, and the comfort of your interview subject. Once you have everything set up, do a test run with yourself or another person so you can tweak and adjust as needed. Make sure you have fully juiced batteries or ample power. Set your alarm if you will need to pause the interview to change batteries or download your files. Plan the length of the interview to the amount of battery life or power you have on your camera. Write down the five most important questions you want to ask, as well as a few warm-up questions or cues to get your relative talking. It may sound silly or like a lot of unnecessary work but believe me, when you start recording, you'll be able to focus on the conversation or interview completely, without a nagging worry that the audio will be inaudible.

Finally, do a last check of your setup to make sure you don't inadvertently do anything to distract your interviewee or take him out of the moment. Imagine your grandfather telling the story of first learning to fish from his father, and your cell phone goes off or the battery on your camcorder dies. So too dies the moment. That far-off look in your grandfather's eye will disappear and be replaced by a sharp look in the direction of the camera. Thorough preparation of all the various elements will allow you to be calm and collected, while making for the best possible video.

Location

It's easy to overlook the importance of a great interview setting. Not only do you want it to look great on camera, but you want it to result in the best interview or conversation possible. Try to pick a place that is specific to your interviewee if that is at all possible; otherwise she will have to get used to a different place, which can create walls that take precious interview time to break down. So, if you can, interview your relatives in their own environment, their natural habitat. Interview Grandfather in his woodworking shop or Grandma in her favorite reading chair.

Don't overlook the importance of privacy. Setting up in the living room on Christmas morning might provide some good footage of flying wrapping paper but if you want a heartfelt memory about a first kiss or your mom's thoughts on faith, you will probably be disappointed. Most folks will hesitate to be forthcoming and frank around other people. Depending on the material you hope to discuss, consider setting up a room far away from the maddening crowd that can accommodate you, the camera, and your relative; leave the peanut gallery on the other side of the door. A discreet set has other benefits as well: it will allow you to control more variables such as light and sound.

If you are planning on using one place for all or most of your interviews, go for as much neutrality as you can. Remove knickknacks and distractions to create as spartan an atmosphere as possible. Keep your interviewee focused on you and the subject at hand, not the stovetop or a changing digital picture frame. (That said, it can be nice to supply a prop or activity, such as crocheting that Aunt Martha can work with during the interview. More on that on page 29.)

Lighting

Lighting is an oft-overlooked element of a great video. Do it well and no one sees or notices it; do it poorly and no one can see a thing. You may think you have a good overhead light, but when you play it back, it looks like your dad is in an interrogation room on *Law & Order*. The overhead light creates shadows all over his face. Or it's a sunny day and you wind up being able to see only half of your sister's face as she tries to block the sunlight.

There are things you can do. You can't control the lighting outside on a sunny day but you can control the time you shoot and you can take into account from which direction the

sun is coming. If you are setting up for a morning shoot, position your subject facing east and your camera west. That way, he'll get light on his face and you won't be looking into the sun or getting serious shadows. Adjust your angles as the sun moves through the sky. Make sense? If you are interested in shooting video outdoors, remember to look for a place with minimal ambient noise (i.e., stay away from the dog park and the playground).

Indoors, the more light you have, the better. Set lights all around your subject, not just coming from one source or location. If you have a lot of overhead light, for instance, pull in floor and table lamps so you have more ambient light coming from below and the side. Turn on all the lights and do a test run, zooming in on your subject. Adjust the position of the lamps until you get great, glowing lighting on the face.

If you want to invest in more lighting, you can purchase inexpensive lighting kits online or in large department or electronics stores. They come with tripod stands and softboxes or diffusers that allow light to disperse evenly on your set. I've even seen people set up white sheets in front of their equipment to soften and spread the lighting. Just remember, the more light you have, the more expression you will be able to capture.

 Sound

Like everything else, test out the audio prior to your interview. Place the camcorder at different distances from the subject, in a closed room, in a noisy room, and so on until you fix upon a position that offers clear audio at a reasonable volume. Ideally, test the camcorder by replicating the conditions of the actual interview space as much as possible. If you have a quiet relative, you might try testing the camera at close range. You don't want to be surprised after the interview to hear that you've only captured mumblings.

While the mic that is built into your camcorder may prove sufficient for your needs, a sound editor I know recommends purchasing an external mic; this way you have a backup audio track and you can play with the sound levels separate from the video. You can purchase a small lavaliere microphone that clips to your interviewee's shirt or a separate mic that attaches to a boom or stand. The latter can be positioned in the precise direction and at the proper angle to pick up your interview subject while eliminating road sounds, the next-door neighbor, a barking dog, etc. You have only one shot to get someone to share a story for the first time, and it would be a shame to record it with shoddy audio. If you are using only the built-in mic on your camcorder, do your best to *soundproof the room.* Hang cloths on walls, close off the area, and place foam, fabric, and other objects around the room to absorb the ambient noise. You don't need to spend a lot of cash to get great audio, but you may have to get creative.

Composition

It's time to free up your inner interior decorator or set designer. With a "less is more" philosophy, cast a critical eye at the space you're planning on using for your interview. You probably don't normally notice the stack of books on the table or the silk flowers on the counter. They are just part of the background of your family's life. But as a director, you should look through the lens with an eye toward composition. Remove extraneous objects and even furniture. Just because that end table has been there since the dawn of man doesn't mean it should clutter up your shot.

Take a note from photographers and think about the rule of thirds. In your mind, vertically divide your screen into thirds and think about placing your interview subject in one of those pieces. I personally like things to be off-center so I'd consider positioning the camera so that a relative is in the right or left third and talking toward the other two thirds of the shot. Don't have him looking the other way. He'll not only need room but he should have a bit of space in front of him so the conversation itself has room to breathe.

The rule of thirds works horizontally as well. Mentally divide your screen into three horizontal stripes. Make sure you give your subject headroom in the top third, unless you're going for a tight shot to capture a particular emotion. If you do that, be sure to zoom out again after the moment has passed. If you pay attention to it, you'll notice that it's very uncomfortable to watch extreme close-ups for any length of time. The interviewee looks trapped.

When setting up your shot, think about the height of your interviewee. If he is approximately your height, it will be easy to set up the tripod properly. If he is a bit taller or shorter, you may have to adjust when he sits down for the interview. It's nice to see a full frame and

Beyond the Family Tree

surroundings initially but when shooting someone sitting, frame him from the chest up. If he's standing behind a counter or table, be sure to include a bit of the furniture in front of him. You'll be able to capture hands and gestures quite nicely and it won't look cut off.

⇨ Your Interview Subject

That brings us to the interviewee. You've done an amazing job preparing the set and an environment conducive to a fun, insightful conversation. The only remaining wild card is your relative. Someone who is bawdy and outrageous might clam up when he sees the red light of the camera. Another might start yammering on about something and completely derail your line of questioning. *Don't panic!*

Comfort is key. You want your relative to focus on the questions or memories at hand, not the environment. Think about what will loosen up family members, be it their favorite alcoholic beverage (just *one* to take the edge off) or cup of tea, holding a sleeping pet, or knitting. Sit them down in a favorite chair or room, set their favorite drink or a pitcher of water nearby. Heck, put out a plate of homemade cookies if you know your brother has a sweet tooth. You'll give him a jolt of energy and he'll appreciate the gesture. Make sure the room temperature is comfortable (those extra lights can make a person sweat). Help your subjects ease into their comfort zone so they will be more fluid and accommodating during the interview. They have to be comfortable enough to answer the uncomfortable questions.

Another thing you might want to consider is having a relative walk you through a signature dish or activity. This would be a wonderful way to pass down beloved recipes or crafts while capturing the essence of your loved one. You never know when you might want to can tomatoes or try your hand at making the family rum cake. An instructional video would be just the thing to refer to. If you *do* plan on recording a demonstration, prepare a few questions that you can pepper throughout the steps so you are capturing memories, anecdotes, and opinions in between the tutorial. And do your best to be fluid. If your aunt is rolling out dough in a manner you've never seen, ask her why she's doing it or who she learned it from. You might find some richness in the minutiae.

WELCOME
TO
OVERLOOK POINT
ROADSIDE PARK
Provided For Your Pleasure By The People Of
MADISON COUNTY
• Please Help Keep The Park Area
• Prevent Forest Fires
• Drive Carefully At All Times

chapter 2

Interviewing *101*

Now that you have your equipment squared away and your set prepped, it's time to think about the actual interview. Remember that this is a conversation. Even if your relative is doing most of the talking, consider that this is a two-way dialogue. It takes the pressure off both sides if you go into it with that in mind. True, you want to capture great footage of your relative telling great stories, but you are there as well. Let yourself be engaged by the interview; respond or ask follow-up questions if something piques your curiosity. But like any conversation, let the other person talk. Let him tell the story the way he wants.

⇨ Plan ahead

Before interviewing a relative, come up with a broad idea of topics you'd like to discuss. To cover all the topics set forth in this book, you'd need a few weeks and a whole lot of memory to store or even process the video or audio recordings. So it's in everyone's best interest for you to come in prepared and focused. Think about your relatives' interests, any holes in their personal history that might yield rich stories, and their own family or love life (depending on their age).

Let's consider the *grandparent interview.* A grandfather might have always seemed old to you but at one time, even he was a young whippersnapper. In his day, he might have been a hell-raiser, a ladies' man, or a pious and hard-working lad. Ask him about what he did for fun as a teenager, what subjects he liked in school, what he wanted to be when he grew up (and how that worked out for him), or his first kiss. Believe me, the stories that will tumble out of him will surprise you. The life he has led might amuse, awe, or just dumbfound you, but it will almost certainly shock you. If your grandfather was a farmer like mine, you might want to ask what it was like living on the farm in the 50s, have him describe a typical day, what he misses most, who his friends were—you get the idea.

Now in contrast, you might also like to interview your ten-year-old niece, who is a chatterbox and total goof. It might be hard to rein her in but that's okay. Giving her a topic and letting her run with it might prove to be high comedy. After all, she hasn't had the time to acquire as many meaningful memories. But she may have other things to bring to the interview table. If she's a ham, ask her to show off her latest dance moves or reenact her favorite movie scene.

She'll be appreciative or perhaps embarrassed when you show this footage to her fiancé someday.

The goal, however, is not to churn out loads of *America's Funniest Home Videos*. You want to capture personal and family history in these interviews. Opt for opinions and anecdotes; find out how your family members feel about things, rather than asking Uncle Scott to show off his uncanny ability to stuff a fist into his mouth. *That* you can send off to a TV show.

If appropriate, *pair up relatives.* Some of my best footage involves my mom and stepdad talking about their first date. What were the important and salient points to Jim (a salt-of-the-earth type of guy) were not what my mother (a more genteel gal) remembered. Having a couple play off each other can make for priceless footage. Think of the sweet and sassy interviews interspersed throughout *When Harry Met Sally. . . .* Interviewing a couple of family members can not only reveal memories and anecdotes, but also showcase their interaction and dynamic in a way that a single interview can't.

Beyond the Family Tree

⇨ Create an Interview Outline

Part of the preplanning should be to focus on a few subject areas, with a select group of questions. Peruse the list of questions in the next chapter and pick out about twenty to twenty-five that speak to you and that you think will cause your relative to open up and dish. What do you really want to know about this particular relative? For a grandparent, it might be more about childhood. For a sibling, memories of earlier days are maybe not as interesting since you were probably there. Instead, ask about your brother's political views or relationship with his new wife. Keeping the list short and focused will prevent you both from becoming overwhelmed with the potential enormity of the interview. Treat it as the first installment, with a plan to continue the conversation another time.

Create a rough outline with the topics you want to cover. List a few questions under each topic heading. If you are going to stay on one topic, just type up a laundry list of questions. It's helpful to put them in a sort of order. For instance, if you are talking about pop culture and the arts, group all your TV questions together before moving on to music or books. It helps both you and the person you're interviewing stay focused and thoughtful.

It goes without saying, but tweak the questions. If a relative is retired, change some of the work questions to past tense. If she is still in college, switch to present tense. These questions are intended to start a conversation or, better yet, spark your own line of questioning.

START OFF SLOW

When getting under way, don't dive in. Give your interview subject a general idea of what you're going to do and what you hope to accomplish. Folks appreciate direction up front and this may save you from having to stop during the interview to offer pointers.

To start, throw relatives some easy questions that they'll have a ball answering. Maybe these are of stories you already know but are worthy of being recorded. For instance, I know my stepbrother Jay is a huge Chicago Cubs fan so I started there. What was his most memorable moment as a Cubs fan? Did he ever skip school or break the law in the name of the Cubbies? What is the farthest he ever traveled to see a game?

Beginning with questions that give a relative a chance to brag sets them up to shine and come alive. If they have a bowling trophy you've always admired or you know they have an amazing green thumb, start there. It's always going to be easier to talk about the terrific before the tragic.

Now that the conversation is flowing and your brother has forgotten that you have a video camera fixed on him, ask him about what it was like when his wife gave birth for the first time, his favorite music in high school, what he listens to today to get revved up or to wind down. Then you can ask about the afterlife, religion, politics, money—stuff that doesn't always trip off the tongue.

LISTEN

While you want to give a relative space to tell his story or share her thoughts, it's also important to listen. Remember, this is a conversation, not a passive activity for you. If Aunt Jeanne is discussing politics or a hot-button topic, don't let the opportunity to go a bit deeper slip through your fingers. If your brother is finally talking about how devastating your parents' divorce was, keep it going. Ask him how he first heard about the split, whether he felt abandoned, if he was angry. These conversations are about *connecting with family.* Allow the interview to be a way in to a deeper relationship.

Listening also allows you to rein in an interview if it's galloping off in a different direction than you intended. Sometimes this is good, but you'll know the difference. If your stepdad is telling the story of saving for and buying his first rifle, let him go. But if he's telling the same tired rant about a coworker that you've heard at least eleven times, it's fine to bring the focus back to the topic at hand. Wait for him to take a breath and kindly ask him a new question or the same one you started with. If he started to tell a story before getting sidetracked, just bring him back to where he left off. You can always edit out the rant so the interview looks somewhat seamless.

🔖 Proceed with Caution

When you sit down with your relative, tell him that he doesn't have to answer anything that makes him uncomfortable. Be aware of sensitivities when talking about military service, religion, sex, and other hot-button topics. If you want to go there, start with a few neutral questions and gauge your interviewee's willingness to talk and overall comfort level. That said, you'll need to keep your eyes peeled for signs of distress. If he starts answering questions in monosyllables, his tone becomes curt or terse, or his body language tightens up (crossed arms, tapping feet, or agitated neck rubbing, for instance), he's probably not digging the line of questioning. Before you give up, gently ask him if he's doing okay. Say something along the lines of, "You seem to be uncomfortable talking about this. Can you tell me why?" If he says he feels interrogated or just doesn't want to bring up something, apologize for touching a nerve and move onto another area of conversation.

If a relative is not warming to your line of questioning from the get-go, it may be necessary to redirect the interview to get him or her comfortable again. The important thing is that he's talking and believe me, with the questions in this book, there will still be plenty of provocative topics to tackle.

But perhaps you have the opposite problem. Your relative is all over the place, running at the mouth and jumping from topic to topic without completing a thought or staying on topic. Maybe he's distracted by the camera or all the attention being paid to him and this manifests itself with a scattered mind. Take control. Ask an extremely focused question to snap him back to the interview.

For example, if your aunt is talking about learning to bake with her mother, ask her about her mother's signature dish. Ask what she considers the most important thing she learned in the kitchen. Ask whether there was any dish of her mother's that she secretly disliked. Ask about Thanksgiving when she was young: did she help with the cooking? What was prepared? See, you could go in a variety of directions with specific questions, but it's important to think on your feet and keep the directing the interview to your satisfaction. While you should be careful not to cut off a great story, limit the scattershot stories and focus the wandering mind. Like I said earlier, lengthy interviews eat up storage space and they can become unwieldy to edit.

Follow Up

So you've got a list of questions for your family member. Great start! Now comes the tricky part: responding to your interviewee on the fly. I'm talking about follow-up questions. We know you're not Barbara Walters or Terry Gross (and if you are, call me!), so it can be hard to know how to direct the questioning.

If you have specific instances you want someone to talk about, ferret out one story. Prompt them; ask them to elaborate or clarify a point they glossed over. Ask them to slow down and repeat things if necessary.

Try not to ask stand-alone "yes or no" questions. There are plenty of questions in the lists that follow that could elicit a one-word response. However, I included those, trusting that if you get an answer, you will follow it up with another question. For instance: If you ask, "Do you regret any relationships?" and the answer is yes, ask your relative to elaborate or share his regrets. A few perfect follow-up questions or comments:

"Tell me more."

"What relationships do you regret being in? Getting out of?"

"What was it in particular about that relationship that you regret?"

"Do you regret causing someone hurt? Being hurt?"

"What do you wish you had done differently?"

"Why?"

Even a simple "why?" can be a compelling and perfect follow-up. Don't settle for the short answer; the longer one is almost always worth drawing out.

Armed with this information, let's move onto the next chapter and the questions themselves so you can plot out some interviews that are sure to spark a conversation, both on and off camera.

The Questions

Finally, we get to the fun stuff: asking thoughtful and often-overlooked questions of your kin. Questions of every kind are sorted by category and are meant to spark both memories and dialogue. You'll find that the stories that emerge are not just one relative's personal history; they are the threads that create your family's tapestry. Don't believe me? Consider this: if your grandfather never met your grandmother, you wouldn't be here. Their story is also your story. Don't you want to know it? Of course you do. But where do you start? How do you draw these rich memories and anecdotes out of your family members?

It seems like an easy task, picking a topic and asking your relative a few questions. But once you cajole him and get him in the chair, *you* might be the one tongue-tied. Preparation of your equipment and your interviewee is critical, but so, too, is it necessary to prepare yourself with a smart line of questioning.

In the following pages you'll find loads of questions, arranged by topic. Use these as a guide for your conversation. Pick and choose from them or use one to jump-start a whole line of storytelling. One simple question might cause your mother to go down memory lane and stay there for quite some time.

In this case, forgo the prepared questions and stay with her on her trip; she'll find stories to share that you never imagined asking. She might direct the conversation for a while as she thinks back on ideas or memories that she hasn't reflected on in quite some time. Use this as an opportunity to create a new shared experience with her as she divulges intimate thoughts or nearly forgotten memories from a far corner of her mind. I bet that with a bit of reflection, she'll remember that boy who made her swoon one summer or the details of her prom dress. And who wouldn't want to know that?

♥ RELATIONSHIPS

Topics don't get much more rich than love and relationships. It's the juicy stuff that makes life full, rewarding, and downright magical. It can also be the cause of heartbreak and grief.

As such a powerful (and perhaps loaded) topic, relationships are the logical place to start your investigation into your family's lives. With a little prompting, you can get a relative talking about love, both true and transitory, platonic and romantic. Family members will happily talk about friendships with important people from the past and present. Most likely, they will be pleased to share the obvious about their romantic relationships. But don't assume that your parents' and grandparents' romantic lives began and ended with each other. *They were people before they were husbands and wives,* and that probably means they had crushes, sweethearts, and heartaches before their respective spouses entered the picture.

Think about it this way: when you reflect on your life, what important stuff would you want people to know about? Would it be how hard you worked at your job? The things that rile you? Or would it be the relationships and people who have shaped and affected your life (and vice versa)?

In my family, the story went that my mom showed up to meet my dad for their first date and he was wearing a velvet smoking jacket. This is hilarious in itself but when you know that my dad was a farmer's son and was greeting her at the door of his family's clapboard farmhouse, it just gets better and better. It begs a few questions. Why did he think that was appropriate date-wear in the mid-60s in rural Michigan? Perhaps more importantly, where did he get a velvet smoking jacket? Is this story even true?

Turns out it was. I asked both Mom and Dad (now divorced) about this. Dad was a bit coy when I asked him whether the story was true. "It might be." (If there was ever a time for a follow-up question . . .) I also wanted to know how my parents met, as well as how they met their next spouse, my stepmother and stepfather.

The tale of how my mom met my stepdad, Jim, is also pretty great. She was working as a waitress and met Jim when she got off her shift and was having a drink at the restaurant's bar. He invited her to his place for breakfast and she agreed, after making sure he had coffee, juice, eggs, bacon, and toast on hand. Remarkably, he did (he doesn't strike me as someone who values a stocked pantry). The next morning, she drove back to his place and left flowers at his door with a note that said, "No man has ever made me breakfast. Has any woman ever given you flowers?" The rest is history.

I didn't necessarily ask to hear all of this, but I realized, with the camera turned on them as they took turns filling in the story details, that this was good material. It was funny and real and rich.

When I asked my siblings and cousins to tell me about their relationships, I was met with little resistance. When my brother John described his first date with his wife, he told me how they had a late-night date when they both got off work (he was working as a card dealer in Reno and Edy was in a band). They stayed up until the wee hours talking and eventually moved the conversation to her car, where John proceeded to rifle through her glove box when he had a private

moment. He nonchalantly told me that he does this regularly, as it can reveal a boatload of information about a person. *Hmm, crafty.*

John gave up his story immediately; this event set him on a path to a happy marriage with a woman he loves. Why wouldn't he want to share it? People love their friends, family, and significant others so this is a pretty easy topic get into, even if you ask questions about past loves, broken friendships, and heartbreak. Just take care not to ask your cousin about his marriage if his wife just filed for divorce. Sensitivity should always rule the day. If you sense someone is tearing up, clamming up, or looking pained, gently ask why he or she is so emotional (your relative might need to talk to someone or you could unlock a beautiful story that has been tamped down for years). If he or she doesn't want to talk, move on to another, less-touchy subject area.

Have you ever had your heart broken?
If so, what happened?

notes

How many times have you been
in love?

Hypothetically speaking, describe
your perfect date.

Tell me about the best date you've
ever been on.

Tell me about the first date with your
spouse/significant other.

Have you ever dated the same type of
inappropriate person over and over?

What do you enjoy about being
unattached? What do you miss?

What do you enjoy about being
attached? What do you miss about
being single?

Do you believe in love at first sight?
Have you ever experienced it?

Have you ever dated someone who
really was unsuitable or just bad news
all around?

Who's the one you let get away? Who let
you get away?

RELATIONSHIPS

notes

Do you regret any relationships?

Have you ever played matchmaker?
If so, how did it turn out?

Are there any friends you have wanted
to break up with over the years?

Have you broken off any friendships?
How did you do it?

What friends drive you nuts?

What friends do you consider like
family?

Who's your oldest friend?

Describe your biggest falling out with
a friend or family member.

What would you want people to say
about you after you're gone?

Describe what you think makes a
relationship work.

What do you think ruins a relationship?

What's the most passionate argument
you've ever been involved in?

Has being honest ever cost you a
friendship?

Who can you always rely on to cover your back or be completely honest?

notes

Do you have a best friend? If yes, what do you love most about him or her?

Have you ever kept a secret from someone and you wish you hadn't?

Have you ever told something to someone you love that you wish you had kept to yourself?

How do you placate or calm your spouse?

What does your partner do to appease you or bring you out of a bad mood?

What terms of endearment have you been called throughout your life?

Share your engagement story.

How did you meet your partner?

How do you keep romance alive with your spouse/significant other?

Did you ever consider marrying someone else?

How do you think life would be different if you weren't with your significant other?

notes

If you're single, how do you think your life would be different if you were married?

Did you ever resent having to change your lifestyle or relocate because of your spouse's job?

What is the biggest challenge of sharing your life/living with someone?

If you're single, what do you envision the hardest thing about living with someone would be?

What is your favorite physical feature of your significant other?

What physical feature of yours do you think your spouse loves the most?

What is the one thing that you wish you could change about your relationship? Your significant other?

What do you think your spouse wishes he/she could change about *you*?

Is the person you are with the person you imagined you'd end up with? If not, describe who you thought you'd wind up with.

Do you ever experience a power struggle in your relationship? What are the hot-button issues?

notes

What favorite song, movie, or TV show of your spouse do you really hate?

What is the best gift you've ever received from your spouse or partner?

When did you know your spouse/ significant other was the one?

What makes your relationship tick?

What does your spouse or significant other do that sends you over the moon (a glance, a term of endearment, a thoughtful gesture, etc.)?

What do you think is the most important quality in a friend? A partner?

Tell me about your honeymoon. Was it everything you hoped for?

If you could spare no expense, describe your dream honeymoon.

Who brings out the best in you?

How do you and your partner split up chores and tasks?

RELATIONSHIPS

notes

What do you think are your and your partner's individual strengths and weaknesses?

How do you handle finances? Joint checking account? Taxes?

Have you ever hidden a purchase from your spouse?

Do you keep things from your spouse? What sort of things do you fail to disclose?

What is the roughest patch you've gone through with your partner? Why do you think it was tough?

What is the worst punishment you've ever inflicted/received?

Describe your marriage proposal.

Did you have a long engagement?

Did you spend a long time planning your wedding?

Was your wedding everything you had hoped for?

If you could go back and change anything about your wedding, what would it be?

Do you and your partner have "a song"?

What song did you dance to at your wedding?

Do you remember your wedding vows?

How did you feel the morning of your wedding day? The morning after?

What was the most stressful aspect of your wedding?

What's your favorite family activity?

What's the most hurtful thing you've ever said or done to a loved one?

How do you apologize when you screw up?

Do you feel you have a dysfunctional relationship with anyone?

Have you ever been in a wedding party that you really didn't want to be involved in?

Did you and your partner ever have a period where you tried to get pregnant without success?

Did you always want children?

notes

RELATIONSHIPS

notes

How did you find out you were going to be a parent? How did you feel?

Did you have any food cravings while pregnant?

How did you figure out the names for your children? Was there a lot of debate? Runner-up names?

What did your older kids think when you brought a new baby into the mix?

Describe your relationship with your siblings. How has it changed over time?

Have you ever openly defied someone in your family?

Have you ever been jealous of someone in your family?

Do you disapprove of a sibling or parent's lifestyle? If so, have you ever addressed it openly with him or her?

Describe a conversation where you felt completely connected to the other person.

Is there any relationship that has ended that you miss in your life?

What is your biggest daily challenge when it comes to living with someone?

notes

Which friend or relative do you wish you lived closer to?

Which relative would you choose to be stranded with on a deserted island?

Who is your most loyal and supportive family member?

Who do you consider your funniest relative?

Have you ever contemplated exploring a relationship with a gender different than your usual preference?

Has a relative ever created a scene at a family gathering?

Have you ever confronted a family member in a way that turned ugly?

Have you ever stopped talking with a relative for a long period of time?

Which relative do you wish you knew better?

Which relative do you see way too often?

YOUTH

Sadly, childhood is often a topic lost to time. Memories of our youth are usually the most treasured, but as we grow into adults, pressing concerns and current happenings tend to eclipse conversations about our childhood. Don't let that happen. Turn back the years as you turn on your video camera.

Think about your own childhood. Even if you're a college student, chances are you don't remember a lot from your early years and sometimes your memories differ slightly or significantly from a sibling or parent. About ten years ago, I wrote down a lot of small memoir vignettes of growing up in Michigan. I laid out the text beautifully and had it printed and bound up for my brothers and mom. I thought the stories were quirky and often funny.

My family had a different take. While I attempted to put a wry take on my parents' divorce and the ensuing years, my brothers found it a tough read because they hadn't known up until then the details of what I went through. My mother felt a lot of guilt over the situation.

Despite the sadness, the little book was ultimately a great thing. It allowed me to record my memories before they were lost to time or blocked out and it opened a dialogue with my family.

Talking about childhood can be a really playful interview topic. However, it can also lead to touching or touchy stories that can shed a lot of light on what shaped your relatives' opinions and personalities. Trauma is magnified as a child so even a story about a "harmless" prank or teasing can reveal deep-seated feelings. My brothers used to tease me mercilessly (or so I thought), nicknaming me "Heifer Head." Not exactly what a young girl insecure about her appearance really wants to hear. It's no wonder I stayed in my room, reading Nancy Drew mysteries and wishing I was a beautiful teen detective with a convertible, not to mention an only child.

This is an excellent topic for letting your interview subject lead the conversation. *Let their stories prompt your follow-up questions.* Asking about your dad or grandfather's childhood chores might lead you to learn all about life on a rural farm in the 40s and 50s. No need to move on to talking about his high school chums until you let him discuss plowing the fields, migrant workers, or keeping the livestock warm in the frigid winters. Or maybe your mom grew up in the 70s and 80s. What a great opportunity to find out what it was like to hear Madonna for the first time or what sort of fashion victim she was in junior high. Stay with a line of questioning until you feel as if you got all the juicy, vivid, and/or tragic details.

Who was your best friend in elementary or high school? Are you still in touch?

Who was the person you wanted to be friends with in high school?

Who was the person you most disliked in high school? Why?

Describe your circle of high school friends.

Did you bully anyone as a kid? Did anyone bully you?

Did you ever get into a fight?

Did you ever tell a boy or girl that you liked him or her? What was the reaction?

Describe your first kiss. Who was it with? On a scale of one to ten, how was it?

Who was your first boyfriend or girlfriend?

notes

YOUTH

notes

Tell me about your high school
sweetheart.

Who were your crushes in junior high
and high school?

Did you ever have a crush on any of
your siblings' friends or your friends'
siblings?

Talk about the first date you ever
went on.

What was a school dance like
for you?

Did you go to prom? If so, describe
your outfit (or supply a photo!).

Did you play any sports in high
school? What was your favorite? Were
you any good? Did you or your team
ever win any trophies?

In which extracurricular activities,
if any, did you participate in high
school?

Were there any clubs or sports
that you desperately wanted to
be part of?

Were you in a clique? Did you want to
be in one?

YOUTH

Were there any embarrassing school portraits? May I see them?

notes

What was the most humiliating thing that happened to you in junior high or high school?

Did your parents ever embarrass you in front of your friends?

What was your favorite song as a teenager?

As a teenager, where did you like to hang out?

What fashion trends do you *really* wish you had ignored?

What was your favorite going-out outfit in high school?

Did anyone ever ridicule your clothes in junior high or high school?

Describe or supply a photo of the most tragic haircut you ever had.

Were you an early or late bloomer?

Did you ever pass notes? Do you remember any of them? Did you ever get caught?

notes

Were you ever in a school play? If so, describe your role and how you got into character.

When did you take driver's ed? Describe the experience.

Did you ever fantasize about any celebrities when you were a preteen? If so, who?

Did you have any posters of celebrities on your bedroom wall?

Did you ever T.P. anyone's house?

When did you first try alcohol?

When did you try your first cigarette?

Did a teacher ever punish you in front of your classmates?

Were you ever a teacher's pet?

Would you consider yourself a brownnoser in school?

What was the worst school lunch you ever had?

Tell me about your best childhood birthday.

As a kid, what was the best gift you received from a sibling?

notes

What was the worst gift you ever received from a family member?

What was your most precious belonging as a kid?

Did you have any imaginary friends?

What is your first memory?

What was your favorite board game as a kid?

Did you have any special skills that you liked to show off?

Would you say you were a daredevil or a bookworm or both?

What was your favorite toy?

Do you have any of your childhood toys?

Did you get an allowance as a kid? How much was it and what did you have to do for it?

What was the first thing you saved up for?

YOUTH

notes

What was the first record,
8-track, cassette, or CD that you
purchased?

What was your favorite TV show
as a kid?

Were there any TV shows you watched
as a family?

Were you scared of the dark?
If so, did you have any bedtime
rituals? (Are you still scared of
the dark?)

Did you ever catch your parents in an
intimate moment?

What was your childhood bedroom
like? Did you have to share a room?

What was your favorite part of the
house you grew up in?

Describe a favorite family pet.

How did you learn about the birds and
the bees?

How did you get your name?

Did you ever send away for something
or join a club without your parents'
permission?

What did you hide in your room?
Did your parents ever find any of your
contraband?

Which friend always seemed to get
you in trouble?

Describe any awards or contests you
won as a kid.

What was your favorite thing to do
when playing by yourself (reading,
building a fort, playing with dolls, etc.)?

What magazines/books did you read
as a kid or teenager?

What were your favorite comic book
characters?

What are some of your more
memorable Halloween costumes?

What was the best sleepover or
slumber party you ever hosted or
attended?

Was there ever anything you really,
really wanted but that your family
couldn't afford?

Did you ever go on a field trip or
school trip? Please describe your
favorite one.

notes

notes

Is there a movie or book that sums up your childhood or teenage experience?

What was your favorite playground activity?

What was your favorite kid snack?

Did your siblings ever tease you? Did you tease them?

Did you have any recurring dreams or nightmares as a kid?

What were your chores?

How often did you see your grandparents? What was a visit with them like? Was there anything you enjoyed doing at their home?

Was there anything you wanted to change about your physical appearance when you were young?

What did you try to talk your mom into buying when you went shopping with her?

Did you ever rifle through your parents' drawers?

Did you ever play dress-up with your parents' clothes?

Did you ever go to sleepaway camp?

notes

Were you ever in Cub or Boy Scouts, Brownies, or Girl Scouts? What was that like?

Did you have four seasons where you lived? How did you play outside in the summer and the winter?

Whom did you idolize as a kid?

Do you remember your mom or dad getting really angry? Do you remember why?

What's the worst punishment your parents ever inflicted on you? What did you do to merit it?

Were you ever spanked as a child? Do you remember why?

What song or album did you play over and over as a kid?

Did you ever swipe cash or spare change from your parents?

What was your favorite kid candy?

📖 EDUCATION AND CAREER

You might assume that talking about work is the last thing a relative might want to get into. But you might be surprised. Think about it. We spend a good percentage of our lives working, sometimes for the weekend, sometimes for the man, sometimes at something we love. Regardless of whether we adore or loathe our job, however, we can certainly talk about it.

To this day, I'm not exactly sure what my dad did at his factory job with Bendix Brakes. It had something to do with the car industry and fixing machines. I *think*. As a kid, every time (which wasn't often) I asked him what he did, I sort of glazed over halfway into the answer. I was probably more interested in my Charlie's Angels Treehouse Hideaway. And I probably asked the wrong question. An open-ended question like "What do you do?" might lead to a vague, open-ended answer. Instead, I'm now employing more targeted questions to get a better overall picture of someone's work life. I might not be enthralled by my dad describing a machine that always broke down, but I'd be spellbound if he started telling me about the various characters he worked with through the years, or about his various jobs as a kid and teenager working for my grandfather on the farm. That would be a rich vein of conversation, indeed.

Similarly, *talking about a relative's schooling can tap into all sorts of memories.* College is often one of the most rewarding and mind-blowing times in someone's life and talking about classes, football games, and late-night debates is something folks are usually thrilled to share. But perhaps school was tough for someone in your family. Maybe they dropped out of high school or had a learning disability that wasn't really addressed. Or maybe they worked their way through high school and college, or entered the workforce as soon as they had their high school diploma in hand. Super! Not necessarily a great experience for them at the time, but this is the sort of anecdote that reveals your relative's mettle or the circumstances that shaped the person he or she is today. Both of my brothers went into the military after high school, so I'd focus on their early schooling, asking about their favorite classes and teachers. But I am also interested to find out what sort of class or training they really enjoyed after they enlisted. Is boot camp really as bad as I think it is? What sort of specialty training did they receive? What were the conditions at the base and in the field like? Did they ever regret their decision to join the armed forces?

There are loads of fun and intriguing questions in this section and I encourage you to stay with this topic for a while and riff off questions depending on your interview subject. I guarantee the payoff will be fascinating and well worth it.

What was your favorite subject in school?

What was your worst subject?

Who was your favorite teacher? Why?

Who was your least favorite teacher?

Describe one of your favorite or biggest school projects.

Have you saved any of your schoolwork?

What's the worst report card you ever received? Did you ever try to change a grade or hide your report card from your parents?

Tell me about your college experience.

What was your toughest college course?

notes

EDUCATION/CAREER

notes

Have you ever pulled an all-nighter? What for?

How do you deal with school or work stress?

Do you think you're good at juggling a lot of coursework or job responsibilities, or are you better focusing on one thing?

In college, did you ever explore majoring in something else?

Did you ever contemplate dropping out of school? Did you?

Did you hold down a job during college?

What part of your education do you think has continued to benefit you in the working world or the "real" world?

What was the most interesting college course you ever took?

Do you ever wish you had pursued an advanced degree?

Did you ever have dress codes in school?

Did you ever cheat on homework or an exam? If so, were you ever caught?

Did anyone ever try to cheat off of you?

notes

What's your most effective study technique?

Do you have any tricks for staying awake in class or a meeting?

Can you study or work with the TV or stereo on?

What music do you like to study or work to?

Who was your best study buddy? Worst classmate to study with?

Did you go away to school or live at home?

What was your school known for?

Did your college have a strong sports program? Do you remember any significant games?

Were you a big sports fan in high school or college?

Describe the most outrageous college party you ever went to.

What was your first job as a kid?

EDUCATION/CAREER

notes

What was your first job out of school?

What did you want to be when you grew up?

As a kid, did you ever envision that you'd be doing what you're doing?

How did you decide on the career you went into?

Are you able to forget about work when you come home?

Have you ever been fired from a job?

Have you ever had to fire someone?

Have you ever had to go on unemployment?

Describe your most difficult boss.

Describe your dream boss.

What part-time jobs have you had during your lifetime?

What's the most satisfying part of your job?

What's the worst part about your job?

Have you ever hated any of your coworkers?

notes

Was there any flirtation with a coworker, boss, or employee?

Have you been a manager? If so, do you enjoy being the boss?

Create a job description for your fantasy job.

Do you feel fairly compensated for your work?

Have you ever gotten a job through contacts, networking, or straight-up nepotism?

If you could do anything else, what would you want to do?

What job would you absolutely hate?

What is the stickiest situation you've ever gotten into at work?

When was the last time you were reprimanded and for what?

Have you ever had to take a second or third job to pay the bills?

What was the worst job you ever had?

notes

Have you ever had to wear a uniform or hat on the job?

What is the best/worst annual review you've ever received?

Did you ever get a raise that far exceeded your expectations?

What do you think you *should* be paid for your job?

What was your best-paying job?

What was the lowest wage you've ever earned?

What were pay wages for you when you first entered the workforce?

What was the worst/best job conditions you ever found yourself in?

What's the best perk of your job?

When does time pass particularly slowly or quickly at work?

What distracts you at work?

Who is the most eccentric or just plain weird boss you've ever worked for?

Who is the most generous boss you've ever had?

notes

What annoying habits does your boss have?

Talk about the most raucous office party you've attended.

Have you ever had to swallow your negative feelings to get along with a coworker or boss?

Have you ever accidentally sent an inappropriate e-mail to the wrong person?

What task have you never been able to master?

What do you feel are your strengths or weaknesses on the job?

Have you ever bungled a job interview? Aced it?

What jobs have you really wanted but didn't land?

What jobs did you take even though you weren't exactly excited about them?

Describe the most painful experience you've had quitting a job or giving notice.

EDUCATION/CAREER

notes

What is the most inappropriate thing you've ever experienced/witnessed on the job?

Have you ever gotten embroiled in workplace politics?

Have you ever switched careers, or thought about it?

What do you daydream about when you're at work?

If you have a desk job, what's in your desk drawer?

What's the best part of your work day?

What's your usual work outfit?

Have you ever had a wardrobe malfunction or accident at work?

Do you have a work outfit or piece of clothing that makes you feel powerful and in control?

Have you ever worn something inappropriate to work? Been reprimanded for it?

What do you think makes a good résumé?

Have you ever embellished or outright lied on your résumé?

notes

Have you ever lobbied hard for a job (sucked up, sent gifts and thank you notes)?

Have you ever worked from home? What were the challenges or perks of a home-based job?

What sort of projects or tasks make you lose track of time?

Do you travel a lot for work? What does that entail? Do you enjoy it?

Have you ever gone to any work-related conventions or trade shows? What did you do there? Any serious partying with coworkers?

Have you ever padded an expense account?

Have you ever had a boss or coworker take credit for your work?

If you could change one thing about your job, what would it be?

♫ POP CULTURE AND THE ARTS

I love movies, music, books, magazines, and television. Most people do, or at least they have their favorites. A lot of folks even have mental lists of their preferred things. It's funny. I know so little about my parents' childhoods but somehow I know that my mother loves *The Robe* and at one time my dad considered *Picnic* his favorite film. My brother Chris loves *Pee-wee's Playhouse* and my step sister Amy and I share a love of Bon Jovi. I think our favorite guilty and artsy pleasures say a lot about who we are, perhaps how we want to be defined. *The Robe* is an inspirational film about the Crucifixion and what came after; for my mom, watching it every Easter has been a ritual that rounds out her holiday experience. As her favorite film, it indicates that she is a sentimental, spiritual person. *Picnic*, on the other hand, is about a drifter who turns a town upside down and then jumps a train to escape from trouble and a small-town life. My dad is a train enthusiast and perhaps this film encapsulates what he loves about Americana and the open rail. Or maybe he just really likes Kim Novak.

My brother has a bit of a childlike sense of humor so it makes perfect sense that he loves *Pee-wee's Playhouse*. If nothing else, questioning your relatives about the media and the arts will provide you with a lot of gift ideas for birthdays and holidays.

This may seem like a sort of lightweight topic. Opposed to Relationships or Faith, it is. But it's a *fun* topic, filled with questions that will engage your relatives. Your cousin will get a kick out of talking about how much she hates musicals and she'll happily open up about her favorite artists. I'm a bit of a pop culture junkie myself so I could yammer on all day about movies, TV, and the lives of celebrities. That doesn't make for a worthwhile interview, however. In the big scheme of things, who cares about the latest Britney gossip? It may be entertaining for a conversation, but not necessarily for an interview. With that in mind, *ask follow-up questions* about *why* your family member fancies or despises the people, places, and things of the art and pop culture world. You might find their answers surprising. Maybe your mother disapproves of Britney Spears, not because of her recent behavior, poor singing, or skimpy clothing, but because she constantly chews gum with her mouth open, supposedly cheated on that sweet Justin Timberlake, or in her first music video, sullied a Catholic schoolgirl image that your mother herself holds dear. If you don't ask specifics, you'll just assume an answer, perhaps wrongly.

What's your favorite book?

notes

Who's your favorite author?

What book have you never been able to finish?

What books do you still want to read?

What is your favorite literary genre (fiction, nonfiction, romance, western, mystery, etc.)?

What is your favorite nonfiction book?

What book do you reread periodically?

What would the name of your autobiography be?

What book(s) have you read more than once?

What book do you wish you could read again for the first time?

notes

What is your favorite quote from a book?

Do you have an idea for a book or screenplay?

What would be the first line of your autobiography?

Is there a quote from a book or film that sums up your life?

What magazines do you subscribe to?

How do you get your news? What's your favorite source of information?

Have you ever read or collected comic books? If so, what are your favorites?

What guilty pleasures do you indulge in (*Desperate Housewives*, bodice ripper romances, Taylor Swift's music)?

What's your favorite movie?

What is your favorite horror, comedy, romantic, science-fiction, western, and period film?

What was the last movie you saw in a theater?

What's your favorite animated movie?

What film genre do you love? Hate?

What was your favorite movie as a kid?

What's the first movie you remember seeing?

What movie have you always wanted to see but somehow never have?

Do you like foreign films? If so, what's the last one you saw?

Have you ever walked out of a movie theater, and if so, what was the film?

Have you ever been to a drive-in theater? If so, what was your most memorable experience at one?

What's your favorite movie snack?

Who's your favorite actor?

What actor would play you in the movie version of your life?

Do you find it easy to remember movie lines or random facts about pop culture?

What's your favorite film quote?

notes

notes

Is there a book or film that you feel captures you or your life in some way?

Has there ever been a world created in film, books, or TV that you wished you could live in?

Who's your favorite classic movie star?

Who is your favorite child star?

When was the last time you went to the theater to see a play? What was it?

Do you like musicals or plays? If so, what's your favorite?

What would others say are your signature dance moves?

What's your favorite TV show?

What is your favorite documentary?

Have you ever considered trying out for a reality show? If so, which one?

What reality show do you tell people is your favorite? Which one *really* is?

Are there any TV shows you can't miss each week?

Are there any TV shows you wish
were still in production?

notes

Have you ever powered through
an entire TV series on DVD in short
order? If so, which ones?

Do you think you watch a lot of TV?
How many hours a week do you watch?

Are there any TV shows you think
are inappropriate or too racy to be
on basic cable?

Do you think there should be
safeguards in place to prevent kids
from watching certain TV shows?

What was your favorite TV show as a kid?

Do you wish you watched less/more
TV? Read more books? Saw more
films? Listened to more music?

Do you enjoy watching awards shows?
If so, what's your favorite? Was
there any acceptance speech that
particularly got to you?

Do you ever watch beauty pageants?
What do you think about them?

Have you ever gotten hooked on a
daytime or nighttime soap opera?

POP CULTURE/ARTS

notes

Have you ever turned down plans to go out because a favorite TV show was on?

Name some of your favorite commercials.

Which celebrities do you find the most attractive?

What celebrity are you surprised is famous or who you think has zero talent?

Which actor, musician, or writer do you think is grossly underrated?

What celebrity do you wish would just go away?

What celebrity can you never get enough of?

Which actor's films will you always go see? Boycott?

Which celebrity's personal style do you admire? Hate?

Which celebrity do you think is overexposed?

Is there any celebrity with whom you are obsessed?

Have you ever met a celebrity? If so, whom?

What celebrity bugs you?

notes

Which celebrity's voice is like nails on a chalkboard to you?

With what celebrity do you actually think you could be best friends, if given the chance?

What celebrity do you think is a horrible person?

Which celebrities are on your "list" (i.e., okay to hook up with)?

Which celebrity do you think is a hot mess on the red carpet?

Who do you think always looks like a million bucks on the red carpet?

Did you ever want to be a performer of some kind? If so, what?

Who's your favorite musician or band?

What's your favorite song?

What songs do you sing in the car? The shower? What gets you going?

What songs do you hate with a passion?

What songs do you know by heart?

POP CULTURE/ARTS

notes

Are there songs that you find hard to listen to because you associate them with people or relationships?

What would be your pick for a song if you had to perform karaoke? Can you give me a sample?

What stations are set on your car radio?

What music puts you in a good mood no matter how down you feel?

Is there a YouTube video that always makes you laugh?

Have you ever posted videos to YouTube? If so, what are they?

What Web sites or blogs do you check regularly?

Do you listen to NPR or talk radio? If so, what's your favorite program or who's your favorite host?

What song lyric breaks your heart?

What song lyric sums up your personal philosophy?

What music do you like to listen to when working out?

Beyond the Family Tree

Have you ever had a commercial jingle stuck in your head? If so, what?

notes

Are there any songs that you frequently can't get out of your head?

What video, computer, or arcade game do you find addictive?

What music has helped you through a difficult time?

What songs do you associate with particular memories?

What music depresses you? Calms you? Energizes you? Arouses you?

Have you ever tried to write a song?

If you could sing like anyone, who would it be?

To which music genres are you most drawn?

Which artists or art periods speak to you?

Who is your favorite artist?

What periods of history are you drawn to, in terms of design? Lifestyle?

☕ FOOD AND DRINK

This is probably a slam-dunk topic for even the most taciturn family member. I mean, who doesn't enjoy reliving an amazing six-course meal, talking about a favorite junk food, or boasting about that scrumptious dessert he or she baked?

Seriously, *talking about food is second only to eating it.* From an early age, taste is a powerful sense. If I didn't already believe this, I had only to watch my friend's two-year-old, who had never had a sweet sugary treat, try her first lemon ice. Piper tore through it in short order, tried to chew the paper, and then screamed for more. The girl apparently has a sweet tooth. Growing up, I can remember the good (Mom's pot roast and cowboy cookies), the bad (the bologna and ketchup sandwiches I loved to pack in my lunchbox), and the ugly (why I couldn't stomach potato pancakes or asparagus remains a mystery). Memories of sitting around the table with the whole family for supper every night around 5 p.m. are still vivid. I remember that my brother Chris loved drinking his 2-percent milk and grossing me out by making faces at me with mashed potatoes in his mouth. We always prayed before dinner, rushing through a blessing in short order so we could start passing the lima beans.

These events weren't isolated; they were connected to life on the farm as a Catholic family. The lima beans were often shucked by me and put in the freezer in the basement for the colder months. The dinner prayer reflected our beliefs and was a nice ritual to start each meal. And Chris's teasing at the dinner table was pretty much reflective of his general hazing practices where I was concerned.

These days, I want to find out my family's most vivid memories of the dinner table and the kitchen, but I also want to know what their current palate is like. My dad, well, he's easy. Give him a bowl of ice cream and he's happy as a clam. But what were his memories around the dinner table when *he* was a wee one? Were there any lean times? Did he ever go hungry? What did Grandma fix him for a special treat? When I asked him about some of this, he told me that a bakery truck used to come all the way from South Bend (which is forty miles away, not an insignificant distance back in the

1950s). While the truck had baked goods, it also carried pints of ice cream. Since the refrigeration in the farmhouse was a bit lacking (or so Dad said), he'd plow through the entire pint in short order so that it wouldn't melt. Some things haven't changed.

The funny thing is that I'm the exact same way. Ice cream is my dietary Achilles' heel and it must be as hard and cold as possible. I can't stand when it starts to melt. This sort of revelation is why I love posing questions to my family. I find a way to further connect, to see the similarities between me and my kin, rather than the many differences. A seemingly innocuous topic like food bonded me to my dad in a way talking about a weightier subject hasn't yet. So don't dismiss this topic; it can wind up revealing a lot about your family and maybe you.

What's your favorite snack food?

notes

Do you snack a lot?

What do you most enjoy about cooking?

What's the first thing you remember cooking all by yourself?

What is the easy recipe you reach for when you don't have a lot of time to cook?

Can you cook? What's your signature dish?

What's the most impressive dish you've ever made? Please share the recipe.

notes

What did you learn from your family about cooking?

What dish do you wish you could make?

If you could learn to cook any cuisine, what would it be?

What technique would you like to master in the kitchen?

What kitchen skills do you wish you possessed?

Are there any dishes you like to prepare that honor your ethnic background?

What foods do you hate?

Do you have any allergies?

What would you like for your last meal?

What three food items would you choose to take with you if you were stranded on a deserted island (assuming an unlimited supply and refrigeration would be available)?

Are there any foods or beverages you can't live without?

What comfort food do you reach for when you're having a bad day?

notes

What food is your weakness?

What's in your fridge right now?

Are there any foods that you regularly binge on?

Describe the best dinner or dinner party you've ever experienced.

Where was the best meal you've ever had?

What is your favorite restaurant?

What's your favorite fast-food restaurant?

Is there any restaurant you'd like to eat at?

Describe the most expensive meal you've ever had.

What's the fanciest restaurant you've ever been to? Was it worth it?

If you could have anyone come and prepare dinner for you, who'd it be?

FOOD/DRINK

notes

What's your favorite type of ethnic food?

Are there any foods you once loved but can't stand to eat now?

What food, dish, or food combination do you love that others would be grossed out by?

What do you like on your pizza?

What's your favorite flavor of ice cream?

What's your favorite sweet treat in the candy aisle?

What's your favorite dessert?

What's your least favorite meal of the day?

Do you regularly eat breakfast? Did you as a kid?

What was your favorite cereal as a kid?

What was usually in your lunchbox?

What was your favorite hot lunch at school? Least favorite?

What dish of your mom's do you crave?

FOOD/DRINK

Did your dad cook when you were growing up? What was his signature dish?

Was there any dish that your mom or dad made regularly that you just hated?

Did your parents ever force you to finish your plate before leaving the table?

Did you have regular family dinners? Any rituals? Prayer beforehand?

Describe a typical family dinner.

Please share memories of a specific meal when you were a kid.

Do you know what your parents', siblings', and children's favorite dishes are?

Was there a food that you ate all the time in college?

What foods do you love/detest the smell of?

What's the worst thing you've ever put in your mouth?

If you had to eat dinner at a convenience store, what would you grab?

notes

FOOD/DRINK

notes

How do you take your coffee?

What food do you love but doesn't love you, if you get my drift?

On a hot summer day, what do you crave?

On a cold winter day, what do you crave?

When you're on the run, what sort of foodstuff do you reach for?

What do you eat when you're dieting?

What do you crave late at night? When you've been drinking?

What foodstuff do you always seek out at fairs, carnivals, or amusement parks?

What, if any, are your favorite cooking or food shows?

Did you ever eat something weird at a friend's house when you were a kid?

What foods do you think sound too weird or gross to eat?

What do you love to eat that other people find strange?

Were you forced to eat something as a kid that you hated?

notes

What foods have you actually spit out during your life?

Who would you invite to your dream dinner party and what would you serve?

What's your favorite kind of birthday cake?

What foods do you associate with different holidays?

What foods do you like to cook on the grill?

What are your favorite picnic foods?

Do you have picnics or eat outside a lot in the summer?

Do you ever stop at farm stands for fresh produce? If so, what fruits or vegetables do you look forward to each season?

How do you feel about buying organic?

Do you try to eat local?

FOOD/DRINK

notes

Do you grow your own produce? If so, what do you enjoy most from your garden?

Do you think you have a green thumb? If so, did you always?

Do you have any gardening tips?

Have you ever canned or put up fruits or vegetables?

What junk food did you love to eat during sleepovers with your friends?

Have you ever played with your food? If so, how?

How do you store your recipes?

Have you ever gone to a U-Pick farm? If so, what do you like harvesting?

How do you deal with hunger pangs?

What is your favorite thing to do with leftovers?

Have you ever tried a fad diet to lose weight? If so, what did you mainly eat?

At what restaurants have you eaten while traveling that you wish were in your hometown?

Describe a meal you've had on the road that hit the spot.

Do you drink? If so, what is your signature cocktail, wine, or beer brand?

What is your first memory of drinking alcohol?

Describe the night where you had the perfect amount of alcohol.

What alcoholic drink does you in every time?

Tell me about your worst drunken experience.

Did your parents drink a lot? If so, do you have any memories of them being drunk?

notes

★ HOLIDAYS AND SPECIAL OCCASIONS

Memories of holidays can go either way. They can be joyous, magical, and downright fun, or a holiday can be a train wreck from the moment it leaves the station. Either way, you win—that is, you as a reporter and interviewer. Family dynamics take front and center during the A-list holidays, and this is an excellent opportunity to really discover what your relatives think about each other, traditions, and the holiday itself.

Perhaps with a bit of inquiry, you'll find out that your mom really dislikes Aunt Dottie's fruitcake but she suffers through a piece every year because she knows it delights Dottie to bring it to Christmas dinner. Maybe she was reluctant to invite Uncle Roger to Thanksgiving because he always showed up sloshed. This might blow your mind now, since as a kid, you just thought he was loud and funny. Maybe your memories of a particular Passover differ wildly from your sister's. It's fun to compare and contrast these events; it will round out and enrich your memories and it will provide a means to deepen your connection with your family.

During one particular Thanksgiving when I was a wee one, I had the chicken pox. What a drag that was. Of course, I still managed to cram in turkey, stuffing, and some pumpkin pie. Another year, our dog Tippy pulled the leftover turkey off the counter and went to town; so much for turkey sandwiches. Sadly, this is about all I remember from each of those holidays. Asking my family for more details or for their recollections will fill in many blanks, and probably be great material on its own.

Take care not to overlook less-popular holidays. My mother is actively involved in the American Legion and is part of the women's auxiliary and the funeral detail, meaning she assists with military burials. She marches in a parade on Memorial Day and on Veterans Day; she cleans soldiers' gravestones and lays wreaths throughout the cemetery. For her, this is as meaningful an experience as any Thanksgiving or Easter.

Start out with the big family holidays and work from there. Just focusing on Thanksgiving, for example, could generate a long conversation about family, food, tradition, and disasters. Holidays can result in *Rashomon*-like re-tellings, with different versions and views of the same event. Perhaps you remember your niece Annie willfully knocking over the Christmas tree, whereas her dad witnessed it as an accident (yeah, right), and Annie thought she was pushed (*please*). Who's to say what the truth is, but it sure is fun to talk about (not to mention, to point imaginary fingers). Use the topic of holidays to recount family gatherings (even if some folks seem misguided in their memories).

What is your favorite holiday? Why?

What do you think is the lamest national holiday?

Have you ever forgotten about a holiday?

What day do you think should be made into a holiday? 9/11, for example? Your birthday?

What holiday tradition do you wish was discontinued?

Do you have any unconventional holiday traditions?

What was your favorite Halloween costume? Please supply a photo!

Do you like to dress up for Halloween? As an adult, do you like dressing up in costumes?

notes

notes

What Halloween candy did you always trade?

Did you ever go to a haunted house around Halloween? If so, what was that like?

Were there any houses on the block that you liked to hit or avoid during Halloween because the offerings were so awesome or lame?

What's your favorite Thanksgiving trimming?

Have you ever had a tense or disappointing Thanksgiving?

Have any family members ever made a scene at Thanksgiving? Was it you?

What was the best Valentine's Day date or gift you've ever had?

Did you ever send a secret Valentine?

Were you ever crushed (or at least disappointed) on a Valentine's Day?

Were you ever pleasantly surprised on Valentine's Day?

Describe your fantasy Valentine's Day.

Are there any holidays you
don't like?

notes

What is the best Christmas present
you have ever received?

What is the worst Christmas present
you've ever received?

When did you suspect Santa was
your dad?

What is your favorite holiday
tradition?

What holiday memory stands out
from your childhood?

Can you remember a favorite gift you
received as a child?

Are Christmas stockings a tradition
in your family? What was the most
unexpected thing you received in
your stocking?

What do you like most and least
about the holiday season?

Describe the worst holiday travel
you've ever experienced.

Does your family have a tree at Christmas? If so, do you get a live tree?

HOLIDAYS/OCCASIONS

notes

Do you have any home recipes to keep a tree alive?

What's your favorite Christmas carol or song?

What is the most you've ever spent on holiday presents in a season?

Describe the best and worst New Year's Eve you've ever had.

Do you make New Year's resolutions? Do you ever manage to keep them?

How do you prefer to celebrate New Year's?

What do you do on New Year's Day?

Did you have any birthday parties as a kid? Any memorable ones?

How did you celebrate your twenty-first birthday?

How did you celebrate your sixteenth birthday?

Has anyone important ever forgotten your birthday?

Do you have a favorite birthday cake or treat?

HOLIDAYS/OCCASIONS

Have you ever been given or thrown a surprise party? Was it a surprise?

What is your best birthday present to date?

Describe your most disappointing birthday.

Describe your most disappointing birthday present.

Who would you invite to your ideal birthday party?

What's the best venue that you've ever celebrated your birthday at?

What is your favorite memory of Memorial or Labor Day? Picnic? Reunion?

Do you do anything on Memorial Day or Veterans Day to honor our armed forces?

Have you ever attended a family reunion?

Would you like to organize a family reunion? Which relatives would you most like to see?

Which relatives would you invite or avoid when planning a family reunion?

notes

notes

Do you have any standing get-togethers with friends or family, like Sunday night dinner?

How do you celebrate Martin Luther King Day?

Have you ever attended any Earth Day events or otherwise celebrated it?

If Jewish, tell me about your bar/bat mitzvah. What's the best one you've ever attended?

What is your favorite part of Passover? Are there any special dishes that you create?

How do you celebrate your anniversary?

Has either you or your partner forgotten an anniversary?

What is the best wedding you've ever attended? What made it so special?

What are your thoughts on bachelor and bachelorette parties? Have you been to any that were particularly memorable?

Have you ever been to a wedding where you knew the couple would eventually get divorced?

Are there any traditions or rituals around baby or bridal showers that you like or dislike?

notes

Have you ever attended a baptism or bris?

What's the best party you've ever hosted?

What do you think makes for a great party?

What qualities do you think are important in the perfect host or hostess?

Do you think etiquette is important? What do you feel is lacking these days when it comes to manners?

What's the best gift you've ever given?

⊤ HEALTH AND THE BODY

Okay, admittedly, this appears at first blush to be the least exciting of the topics. However, asking questions about fitness and health can prove to be a very *practical line of questioning.* Gather your family's health history as you learn about surgeries, ailments, and other health concerns that your family members may have had since you were living in close quarters.

I've always admired my brother John's daredevil spirit. As a kid, I saw him go off with a friend and some homemade skis to fool around in the woods. He returned with a giant gash in his head. Yeah, that required a trip to the hospital.

Then there was the day I dared him to jump off the roof of the shed near our house. Did I mention he's a daredevil? He jumped—and then writhed around on the grass in pain, yelling for me to go find Mom. I just stood there and cried. Eventually I moved, and yep, that broken arm needed to be put in a cast at the hospital.

These days, John has passed on his daredevil genes to his kids and I'm frequently getting updates from the emergency room and the like. We are passing into middle age and our own health concerns have to do with suspicious test results and acid reflux. But even that sort of information can provide a way to connect (not to mention round out) our family's health history. For instance, sharing stories about acid indigestion can reveal a high stress level despite low blood pressure. That might lead to a conversation about the stressors in one another's lives, including family, job, travel, finances, and health. Health can be a springboard into a variety of anecdotes and areas. Discussing a trip to the ER can lead back to a car accident, which was caused by a heated argument, which involved a disagreement about summer vacation plans, which eventually can be traced to financial worries. Look at the wonderful history that can be revealed with a few well-placed questions.

Health touches upon all other areas of life and health issues can color events both negatively or positively. Perhaps your cousin is a breast-cancer survivor and is training for a 5K run (or even a marathon). Talking about her worout regime and diet would be a wonderful way to share her enthusiasm and support her in her quest to be fit and healthy. Don't be surprised, however, if she also asks you to be a sponsor. In fact, once you've interviewed your cousin, posting her video along with details of her run would be a terrific way for your entire clan to get in on her inspiring undertaking. Your interview is not just a historical record or a way to learn about your family; it can also be a marketing tool!

Detail any surgery you've had.

notes

Have you ever been in a position where you feared for your life? If so, do tell.

Are you allergic to any medications? Foods?

How do you stay fit and healthy?

What is your most reliable over-the-counter medication? Prescription medication?

When were you in the best shape of your life?

What is your favorite physical activity? What's your least favorite activity?

Have you ever played any team sports?

Have you ever had the measles or chicken pox?

Describe the sickest you've ever been.

notes

Have you ever broken any bones? If so, describe the circumstances.

Do you have a living will?

Are you an organ donor?

Would you donate an organ to save a relative?

If you needed a transplant, would you ask someone in your family to donate?

What is your blood type?

Do you have any chronic health problems?

Have you ever undergone physical therapy? What was that like?

Have you ever sought out alternative medicines, such as acupuncture or homeopathy?

Do you have any health issues you believe are genetic?

What's the worst accident you've ever had?

Are there any medications that you don't like taking (make you nauseated, dizzy, etc.)?

Are there any medications that you got hooked on (or were in danger of getting hooked on)?

Have you ever taken antidepressants?

Do you generally run hot or cold?

What sort of climate does your body best respond to?

Have you ever taken any yoga classes? What did you like best about them?

What is your worst health fear?

Have you ever looked into ayurvedic philosophy? Do you know what your dosha is? Does it fit you?

Have you ever been in a car accident? If so, describe how you felt as it was happening. Were you or was anyone else injured?

Have you ever injured another person?

Have you ever had any injuries or ailments that changed your appearance?

Do you fear growing old? If so, why?

Do you believe in therapy? Have you ever entered into therapy?

notes

notes

What hereditary illnesses are you afraid you'll contract or develop?

Is there any part of your body you wish you could change?

Do you have any habits or vices you know to be unhealthy? Do you want to quit them?

Are you happy with your appearance?

Did you ever wish you looked different?

What foods make you feel healthy as soon as you eat them?

What compliments or put-downs do you remember someone telling you about your appearance?

What physical attribute are you most vain about?

Are you an early bird or night owl?

How much sleep do you ideally need each night?

Are there any periods during the day where you feel really tired or sleepy?

How do you act or feel when you are sleep-deprived?

How do you combat insomnia?

notes

What makes you feel better when you have a cold? The flu?

Do you have any hangover remedies?

What group sport do you love to play?

How do you alleviate stress?

How do you feel when you exercise?

Who do you think is your most beautiful friend or family member?

Do you like to sunbathe?

Do you think you look better with a tan?

Is there a body part that you can't stand for people to touch?

Have you ever wished for a different hair color or texture?

When have you felt your most attractive?

Have you ever experimented with recreational drugs? If so, which ones? How did they affect you?

Have you ever sat someone down to discuss their drinking or drug use?

📖 FAITH

Religious beliefs are always a slippery slope, no matter how much you agree with another's views. Broaching the subject should always be done in a respectful, curious manner and should—just as importantly—stay that way throughout the interview.

I was raised Catholic but I am not as ardent a follower as I was during my school years at Lake Michigan Catholic High School. My mother turned away from the church altogether, my dad and stepmom embrace it more and more, my brother John became a Latter-Day Saint when he married, and I'm not sure to what level my brother Chris and his family practice. And that's just my immediate family! Because I'm a lapsed Catholic, trying to talk about religion and faith can make my family suspicious of my motives when I ask questions. I think they fear that I'm going to try to debunk their beliefs or engage them in a spirited debate. But I learned long ago that *no one wins a debate about faith.* People believe what they believe and it is best to respect that and try to bridge any religious divide through an exploratory, "I

want to learn from you or at least gather information" position.

My stepmother, Pat, finds a lot of strength, peace, and purpose in her faith. She volunteers through the St. Vincent de Paul Society, helps the less fortunate during tax season, works in the church's community garden, and chauffeurs folks to and from doctors' appointments. She is an incredibly giving person. But she's also deeply spiritual. She and my dad participate in "eucharistic adoration," where the Blessed Sacrament is exposed for twenty-four hours. What that means is every Friday, from 11 p.m. to midnight, my dad and Pat take a shift (that's what I call it), keeping a constant vigil over the sacrament. When I first heard about this (it's one of those things that escaped my attention during religion class), I was fascinated and perplexed. You just sit in a side chapel and guard the sacrament until the next group relieves you? Far out. Of course, I wanted details. Even if this isn't my cup of tea, I respect the ritual and admire the comfort they get from it.

So open your mind and remember that you are going to be info-gathering, not engaging in a philosophical debate. That will just put someone on the defensive, which is the last thing you want here. In fact, with careful, encouraging questions, you might find this to be the richest topic of all. Faith is often so private that when you do talk about it, surprising views surface from people you know intimately.

How often do you pray?

When you pray, do you recite a prayer or make up your own? Talk with God, Jesus, Mary, Allah, a patron saint, etc.?

How do you visualize God?

When you pray, what do you pray for or about? Do you have any ritual around your prayers (same time every day, light a candle, start with a known prayer before personalizing)?

Where is your favorite place to worship?

Was there one sermon or lecture that really affected you?

Has there ever been a time that you questioned your faith?

Were/Are your parents very religious or spiritual?

What do you think is the most important commandment or rule to follow?

notes

FAITH

Have you ever felt the Holy Spirit or another sensation you attributed to something spiritual?

Do you relate to one saint in particular?

Do you have a favorite saint, prophet, or religious figure?

How do you see God in the world around you?

Do you believe in free will, predestination, or something in between?

Have you ever experienced something you thought was divine intervention?

Have you ever experienced something you'd consider a miracle?

Do you believe in miracles?

What is your favorite passage in the Bible, Koran, Torah, Book of Mormon, or other spiritual tome?

To which person do you particularly relate in the Bible, Torah, Book of Mormon, or your sacred book?

If you are Christian, do you prefer the Old or New Testament? Why?

Beyond the Family Tree

FAITH

What faith other than your own do
you feel an affinity for?

What do you believe is necessary for
salvation?

What is your favorite part of your
faith's worship service?

Are there any tenets of your religion
that you don't fully accept or believe?

Have you ever switched places of
worship because you didn't like the
religious leader or the congregation?

How does your faith and practice
today differ from when you were
a child?

How did your parents or grandparents
practice their faith?

Do you believe that prayer can cure
you instead of medicine and medical
treatment?

Are you actively involved in your religious community? Do you volunteer
or help with services?

How important is it that your children
follow your faith? How would you feel
if they turned away from your faith?

notes

FAITH

Are there any times of the year that you have to observe a special diet because of your faith? Do you have any special recipes you can share?

Do you believe in one true faith? That those who don't follow your religion are damned?

Have you ever attended services for a different faith?

Have you ever explored other religions?

Are there any tenets or beliefs from another faith that speak to you?

Do you consider yourself judgmental about religious issues? What do you think of people who don't practice a religion or who don't share your views?

What do you think about atheists or agnostics?

Do you have a favorite religious leader?

What do you think about Darwin's Theory of Evolution?

Do you believe in Adam and Eve?

Do you believe in heaven and hell?

FAITH

If you believe in heaven, how do you envision it? How would you like it to be?

What do you think happens when you die?

When you die and arrive at the pearly gates of heaven, what would you say?

What would you want to be said during your eulogy?

What sort of last rites would you like?

How do you want to be buried or cremated?

Describe how you envision your funeral.

Do you believe prayer can affect change?

Have you ever had your prayers answered?

When do you feel closest to God?

Would you die for your faith?

What do you think about Jesus Christ? Buddha? Joseph Smith? Other religious figures?

What do you think about the history of polygamy in the Mormon church?

notes

FAITH

notes

If you're Jewish, how do you celebrate the High Holy Days?

Do you believe in reincarnation? If so, who do you think you were in a past life? Who would you like to come back as?

Are there any philosophers you agree with? Adamantly oppose?

If you could ask God (or a higher power) a question and get an answer, what would it be?

What do you think is necessary to achieve heaven?

Have you ever helped someone through a crisis of faith?

If you could take any spiritual leader out to lunch, who would it be?

Who is the most spiritual person you know?

Has anyone ever tried to convert you to another faith?

How has your relationship with your faith changed over time?

What is your favorite piece of religious art?

✈ HOME AND TRAVEL

Some of our best memories are tied to a special location. It might be your grandmother's kitchen or it could be a church in Santorini. I find that I have to have trips scheduled to look forward to in order to keep my spirits up in my everyday life. Even if it's a trip home to visit the folks, I need to have something on the calendar.

I don't think I'm alone. Everyone longs to get away, whether it's a little girl wanting to travel to an imaginary Candyland or a retired grandparent, itching to get on the road in a fifth wheel. Asking about travel plans as well as *past adventures* is sure to spark a lively and happy conversation.

When my grandmother passed away, I inherited some of her jewelry. I was curious about a couple of pieces of Mexican silver, and it wasn't until I asked my dad about some photographs from his childhood that I learned they took a trip to Texas, which is maybe where she picked up her pony pin and charming little drop earrings. I had a vision that she had had a dalliance with a dashing Mexican man but I suspect she just got them as souvenirs when she was near the border.

Like many of us, I've been fortunate enough to have traveled quite a bit as an adult. But man, oh man, we hit the road for weeks at a time when I was a kid. We'd pile into a station wagon or van and head out on epic road trips. My dad is an avid train enthusiast and we often traveled along the "old" highway, which is invariably next to railroad tracks. We never stayed in one location for long, my dad preferring to cover a lot of ground in the two weeks he had off from the factory. Consequently, most of my memories of the family vacation involve being carsick in the backseat, playing the license plate game, or trying not to get annoyed with my brothers. However, I do remember the Eisenhower Library and Museum in Abilene, Kansas; hunting for chunks of copper in the river in Michigan's Upper Peninsula; and riding a steam-powered train between Durango and Silverton, Colorado. When talking to my brothers, it's interesting to find out what's on their highlight reel of summer vacations.

For my dad, the answer can be found by looking through his slide collection. After a vacation, we would always be unpleasantly surprised to find ten slides of train engines to every one family member (why we were shocked, I don't know). That's a memory on which my brothers and I are all in agreement.

Regardless of whether there's a train buff in your family tree, there are always great details, anecdotes, and color in talking about a trip taken or dreamed of.

notes

What geographical location makes you most happy? Why?

Is there someplace you were really excited to visit but were disappointed when you finally went there?

Where have you always wanted to visit?

Describe your dream vacation.

Describe your dream weekend retreat.

Tell me about the best trip you've ever been on. Why was it so great?

What was the best family road trip you went on?

What was the lamest family road trip you participated in?

Describe your worst travel experience.

HOME/TRAVEL

What is your favorite airport? Least favorite?

notes

What is your worst experience in an airport or on a flight?

Do you have any rituals or routines when traveling?

What things do you have to put in your carry-on luggage (pillow, drugs, etc.)?

What food from an exotic locale or vacation do you dream about?

What souvenirs do you treasure?

Did you ever play any travel games? What was your favorite?

Was there any trip you dreaded going on?

Where is the most surprising place you've visited?

Have you ever been detained? Banned from a country?

Have you ever made any lasting friends on a trip?

What is the most visually stunning place you've visited?

notes

What places have you visited where it felt like home?

Who's the coolest person you've met during your travels?

Have you ever had a romance or fling while on holiday?

Have you ever taken ill during a trip?

What do you enjoy doing when you travel?

Do you like traveling alone? Have you?

What's the worst lodging experience you've ever had?

What's the best hotel, B&B, or hostel experience you've ever had?

Have you ever been robbed or taken advantage of while traveling?

Have you ever felt as if you were in danger while traveling?

What's your favorite reading material when you're at the airport or on a flight?

What music do you like to listen to while on a roadtrip? During a flight?

HOME/TRAVEL

What's your preferred mode of travel?

notes

Have you ever taken a cruise? Describe the experience.

If you had all the money in the world, where would you want to retire?

If you could travel for a year, where would you go and what would you do?

Are there any countries or regions of the world that you don't care if you never visit?

If you could live in another country, where would it be?

What is your favorite city?

When you visit a new city, what do you like to do?

When you check into a hotel, what is the first thing you do when you get to your room?

Are you concerned with germs when you travel?

Have you ever had to cut a trip short because of an emergency?

notes

Do you have any problems relaxing or sleeping on vacation?

Do you break up your vacation time or save it up to use all at once?

When you were a kid, what was your favorite part of family vacations?

Which friends or family would you most like to travel with?

Which friends or family would be able to communicate and get around easily in a foreign country, no matter the language?

Do you like your vacation to be about adventure or relaxation?

What are your favorite day trips to take on the weekend?

What's your favorite room in the house, and why?

Describe your dream home.

Describe the crappiest place you've ever lived.

Have you ever had roommates? How was that?

How many different places have
you lived? Talk about each move.

notes

Are there any states you have yet
to visit?

Have you ever lived in a place you
believed to be haunted?

What feeling do you try to create
in your home?

☑ POLITICS, LAW, AND COUNTRY

Growing up, we never talked about politics or money around the dinner table. In fact, we didn't talk about politics much at all, except when my dad—a lifelong union guy— would rail about the plight of the blue-collar worker. Consequently, I grew up with undeveloped political beliefs and very little idea of what my parents actually thought about issues and various public servants. Only in the past few years have I gotten up the moxie to ask relatives about their views. It can often raise my blood pressure, seeing as we usually don't see eye to eye, but I've learned to prepare myself for the conversations. And when they say something I don't agree with, instead of changing the subject or blowing up, I go into their beliefs and opinions even more. Just asking, "Why do you think that?" in a nonjudgmental way can yield a lot of conversational fruit.

Politics are inextricably tied to the law, the armed services, and the nation in general. It's particularly wonderful to ask older relatives about their experiences serving in the military; a grandfather may have served overseas or seen battle in a war. He may not have discussed his military service in years; your conversation could allow him to share not only his memories but his views on the current state of world and national affairs. He might be happy to talk about his day-to-day routine, the lousy food in the barracks, and how he spent his weekend when he was granted leave. He might be more reticent to talk about a buddy who died in the field or dropping bombs on the enemy but it's worth gently staying with him on this topic. If he clams up about any question, ask him how he's feeling or what he's thinking. You may not get a lot of details, but you could find yourself connecting with your grandpa in a whole new way.

I find it fascinating to think about my family against *the backdrop of war and politics.* My grandfather served in World War I, staying with a German family in the Black Forest. When he returned to the United States, he sent for the family's daughter. That young unmarried woman traveled by herself across the ocean to join my grandfather and eventually become my grandmother. If it wasn't for war, I wouldn't be here. Sadly, I didn't hear much of this story until my grandmother's funeral. I so wish I had taken the opportunity to ask her if she was scared to travel alone, hesitant to marry a much older foreigner. I would have loved to have known if she was in love with the tall American soldier or if she hoped she would fall for him. Maybe that wasn't even an issue; maybe she knew it was an opportunity for a better life. I'll never know so I can only imagine and hope that she was happy to marry Grandpa and remained happy throughout her life. See what golden nuggets can come out of talking about politics, the law, and the military! Don't wait to chat up an elderly relative; like family, time is precious.

Have you ever served on a jury? If so, do you have any interesting stories as a juror?

Have you ever given an excuse to get out of jury duty?

Have you ever broken the law? If so, what did you do and were you caught?

Which public service uniform do you fancy the most?

How do you feel about the police in general?

Ever seen the inside of a jail cell?

Have you ever been the victim of a crime?

notes

notes

Who did you vote for in the recent election? Are you happy with how you cast your vote?

Do you feel the current elected officials are living up to the promises they made in the last election?

What did you think of how the candidates handled their campaigns in the last election?

Do you pay attention to the polls during an election? How do you educate yourself on candidates and issues?

What is the most important issue when you go to the voting booth? Has that changed over time?

Do you ever decide not to vote? Why?

Do you vote in the primaries or on a local level consistently?

Is there any vote that you've cast that you now regret?

What do you find most aggravating about political news coverage?

Do you feel on top of political and national news? If so, how do you get your news?

Do you follow politics?

notes

Who is your favorite political journalist?

Who is your favorite president or politician?

Which politician do you respect the least?

Which historic events have you witnessed? What affected you the most?

Do you believe in capitol punishment?

Do you always vote along party lines?

Have you ever served in the armed forces? If so, what countries did you go to?

Who in your family has served in the military? Were they drafted? Did they serve during a war?

Did you see any "action"?

Are you still in touch with anyone from your squad or regiment?

What made you want to join the military? Or were you drafted?

POLITICS/COUNTRY

notes

Do you regret any of your time in
the armed forces?

Were you ever frightened or uncer-
tain during your time in the military?

Did you ever silently disagree with
orders from higher-ups?

What was your best experience
during your military service?

Did you carry any special items with
you during your tour of duty?

What was your usual day-to-day
regimen like in the military?

Describe your military uniform, both
fatigues and dress.

Did you ever win any medals or
commendations for your service?

Do you feel our country has a right or
obligation to get involved with other
countries' governments?

Do you feel we should be militarily
involved in other countries' political
unrest?

Do you feel that the United States
should act as the world's police force?

Have you switched political parties?

notes

Do you feel that nuclear weapons should be dismantled?

Do you believe the United States should maintain a strong nuclear weapons program?

How do you feel about the atomic bomb being dropped on Nagasaki and Hiroshima?

Do you feel the use of a weapon of mass destruction is ever warranted?

Do you feel torture is sometimes necessary to preserve national security?

Have you ever attended an inauguration?

Do you usually watch the State of the Union address?

Do you enjoy watching debates?

Are you afraid of anthrax or germ warfare?

How do you feel about the current administration?

POLITICS/COUNTRY

notes

What do you think is the biggest issue facing Americans today?

Do you think health care is a right?

How do you discuss politics in your family?

Do you freely discuss your political beliefs or do you feel that they are private?

📷 LEISURE PURSUITS

Sometimes a family member's hobby is front and center, which may make you overlook some interesting questions. As I said earlier, my dad has been a train enthusiast for as long as I can remember. It colored every family holiday and he spent many an evening squirreled away in the basement working on his miniature train layout. Slides from our summer vacation revealed engine after engine. Needless to say, as a kid, I was *not* enchanted with my dad's hobby.

That hasn't changed. He lives in a different home now, but he still tinkers with his train layout in the basement. He will still speed up on the highway to get ahead of a moving train and capture it on camera. He's currently in the process of digitizing his slides for his/our continued viewing pleasure. But in thinking about this book, I realized that I have been so irritated by his train fascination that I've never bothered to ask about when and why his interest began. That line of questioning might result in insight and understanding rather than the mild annoyance I have felt for decades.

On the flip side, you may only see certain relatives infrequently and when caught up with chit-chat, you may never learn that they have a secret, or at least under-the-radar pastime or skill. Your grandpa might love to sing the blues but never sings in front of people. Your cousin might whittle when he's stressed, or head to the casino on his lunch break, or, gulp, go train-spotting for sheer pleasure. Asking a few questions seemingly *out of left field* might yield more than a few laughs: it might make your loved one open up and talk a blue streak about his secret or not-so-secret passion. This might be one of your easier interview topics; people love to talk about the stuff that juices them.

What would you say is your favorite hobby, craft, or pastime?

Do you have any musical ability? If not, did you at any time think you did?

notes

notes

Have you ever performed in any sort of theater? If so, what were the high and low points?

Can you play an instrument? Did you ever want to learn? If so, what instrument?

Did you collect anything as a kid? Do you still collect it?

What have you made that you're most proud of?

What is the most far-fetched or outlandish thing you've done to follow your passion?

Who shares your love of your hobby or pastime?

How does your family feel about your hobby or passion?

Have you ever become obsessed with a hobby or craft? Series of them?

Have you ever stayed up all night working on a project?

Have you ever done any volunteer work?

Do you believe in any New Age practices, such as Reiki or reflexology?

Do you believe in feng shui, the eastern practice of thoughtful placement of items in a space? What area of your house do you believe has good/bad energy?

Have you ever practiced yoga? If so, what was your favorite aspect of it?

Do you have a blog? If so, talk about it.

Are there any blogs that you read regularly?

Are there any hobbies you'd like to start pursuing?

Do you have any home-improvement projects in the works? Are there any on your wish list?

What clubs, groups, or organizations have you belonged to during your life? Are there any that you wished you had joined?

Have you ever been in a book club?

Is there any club you'd like to start?

Is there a class you're dying to take?

What sort of class would you be qualified to teach?

notes

---

notes

Do you have a close relationship with your car?

What has been your favorite car to own?

Tell me about your first car.

Can you perform any basic maintenance on your car?

If money were no object, what sort of vehicle would you want to own?

If you could be a professional athlete, what sport would you play?

Do you still follow your alma mater's sports teams?

Are you a fan of your local sports teams?

What sports moments still live vividly in your mind?

What's the craziest thing you've ever done in support of a sports team?

Do you go to sporting events regularly?

Who's your favorite athlete?

LEISURE

Do you watch the Olympics?
What moments do you remember
in particular?

notes

Do you follow World Cup soccer?

Have you ever golfed? If so, what was
that like?

**What golf course would you really
love to play?**

Have you ever had a hole-in-one,
or come close?

**Have you ever entered a tournament
or sporting competition?**

Do you like to bowl or shoot pool? Are
you any good?

**Have you ever tried to brew beer
or make wine at home?**

Do you enjoy going to beer or
wine tastings?

**Do you have any artistic ability?
Do you like to draw or doodle?**

What Web sites do you check regularly?

**What is your favorite board game?
Do you play it regularly?**

LEISURE

notes

What is your favorite video game?

Do you consider yourself computer-savvy?

Describe the first computer you ever bought.

How much time do you spend connected to the Internet each day?

What do you like to do in your downtime?

What's your favorite outdoor activity?

Is there any talent you wish you had?

What do you sing in the shower?

Is there anything you'd secretly like to do or learn, but are a bit embarrassed to admit it?

Did you ever try to learn something to impress someone?

Do you enjoy gambling? If so, do you go to a casino regularly?

What do you play when you gamble?

How much have you ever won or lost at gambling?

Do you enjoy carnivals, fairs, and amusement parks? If so, what's your favorite ride?

What's your favorite way to unwind on the weekend?

Describe the most enjoyable Saturday you've ever had.

notes

♀ HOPES, DREAMS, AND DEEP THOUGHTS

Who doesn't like talking about themselves? Seriously? Some people might profess to hate the limelight or shy away from attention, but with genuine interest, most folks will blossom and become downright eager to share personal information, thoughts, opinions, and dreams. This is a great chance to ask fun hypothetical questions, from the expected (What would you grab in a fire?) to the more thought-provoking (If I could put you in a time capsule right now and you could meet your future self at the age of seventy, what would you ask? How would your future self answer?). Did I just blow your mind?

It's also a good place to just ask about someone's favorite things, preferences, and dislikes. We've covered some of these questions in other sections but now is the time when you can let loose and just have fun getting to know your relative in a whole new way. I know that I tend to assume answers instead of asking a person directly for what they think. Maybe your sister's favorite color was pink when she

was a kid and you've been buying her pink sweaters and the like for years. If you step back and ask her what her favorite color is now, as an adult, she might reveal that she OD'd on all things pink around the age of fifteen and now is drawn to earth tones. Don't skip over what you think is an easy question or obvious answer, and you might be enlightened and entertained by your relative's response.

I always want to believe that my mom still has the same style and taste as she ever has. But as she gets older, of course her preferences have changed. She used to love wearing silk scarves and interesting brooches. At the time, she was an antique dealer and it made sense that she dressed with vintage flair. These days, she's retired and travels south during the winter months. Her style is decidedly more dressed down. I've had to ask her what colors she fancies, what garments she finds most useful when she's on the road.

Think about yourself and how much your tastes and ideas have changed over time. It makes sense that answers aren't *set in stone* and evolve as we do. Since we constantly add events and memories, we have to reassess our vices and accomplishments, our hopes and dreams. In talking to our kin, we might find that they've achieved their dreams or have all sorts of new goals. At best, chatting with someone about a dream or goal can help bring it that much more into being. At worst, it provides for an aspirational interview.

Do you have any phobias (fear of heights, snakes, planes, snakes on planes)?

What family mementos or heirlooms do you most treasure?

What is your most precious possession?

If your home were on fire, what three things would you grab (assuming your family and pets got out already)?

What would you say is your personal motto?

Have you ever wanted to change your name? If so, to what?

Do you believe in ghosts or spirits?

Have you ever experienced something you couldn't explain?

How do you feel about death? What do you think happens when you die?

notes

notes

Tell me one thing others would find surprising about you.

What is the thing you did or made that surprised even yourself?

If you won a million tax-free dollars, what would be the first thing you'd buy?

What's your favorite color?

What color do you love to wear?

Describe your all-time favorite outfit.

What do you feel most comfortable in?

How would you describe your personal style?

Do you have a will? What would you put in your will?

Have you ever snooped in someone's medicine cabinet, cupboards, closet, or glove compartment? Learn anything interesting?

Do you have any private habits that others might consider gross or uncouth (do you belch, fart, or spit if no one is looking, for instance)?

Do you consider yourself a neatnik or more of a slob?

Is there any grooming you are obsessive about? Couldn't care less about?

What do you like and value most about yourself?

What are you most proud of?

What are you least proud of?

What are you trying to improve in your life or in yourself?

What would you consider your biggest vice?

Of what quality or vice in others are you the most judgmental?

How reliant are you on your computer, e-mail, the Internet?

What's your favorite mode of communication (in person, phone, e-mail, IM, letter, etc.)?

What would you like to make more time to do?

What are your pet peeves?

notes

HOPES/DREAMS

notes

If I could put you in a time capsule right now and you could meet your future self at the age of seventy, and you could ask yourself three questions, what would you ask? How would you answer? Would your future self lie to you?

Do you have any rituals that you perform daily or regularly, such as checking the door lock several times before turning in or washing your hands incessantly?

What famous people would you like to meet, or have over for dinner (living or dead), and why?

Boxers or briefs?

What nicknames have you had throughout your life?

Have you ever been teased and called something you hated?

What was the hardest thing about living on your own for the first time?

Where do you go when you want to be alone?

What do you wish you had more time to do?

138

Have you ever consulted a psychic?

notes

What is your favorite way to procrastinate?

What Web site, blog, or book do you wish someone would create?

Is there any store where you always go crazy and buy more than planned?

Would you consider yourself more of a dog or cat person? Neither? Both?

In your lifetime, what has been your favorite period?

If you could have lived in any other time, when would it have been?

Do you believe in UFOs, extraterrestrial life, and/or nonbiological life?

Do you consider yourself superstitious? If so, about what? Do you have any rituals (throwing salt over a shoulder)?

Do you know what your Myers-Briggs personality type is? If so, what are the traits?

If aliens abducted you, what part of your body do you think they'd want most?

HOPES/DREAMS

If friendly aliens abducted you, what would you want to teach them?

What is the most expensive thing you've ever bought yourself?

What was the smartest purchase you've ever made?

What purchase do you most regret?

How would you describe your personal style?

What distracts you?

What do you find sexy?

What do you find beautiful?

Describe the best dream or worst nightmare you've ever had.

If you could live during any historical era, when and where would you choose to live?

If you could go back in time, what advice would you impart to your younger self?

If you could be a member of any band, which would it be and what would you play?

If you were to impersonate a celebrity, who would it be?

What is your favorite word or phrase?

What is your favorite joke or riddle?

Do you believe in astrology, horoscopes, palm reading, tarot, and other forms of divination?

Do you feel as if your astrological sign suits you?

Are you attracted to certain astrological signs? Are there any that you know to steer clear of?

notes

👤 FAMILY HISTORY

I was extremely close with my Grandma Worick. We lived next door to her farmhouse when I was growing up in rural Michigan. I saw her nearly every day during those early years. I ran to her house when my brothers wouldn't let me watch *The Waltons* on TV. In the winter, I sat over the register with her, doing crosswords on a TV tray. I joined her cronies for canasta. She fed, entertained, and loved me.

And when she died, I was devastated. I was even more gutted at the funeral, when cousin Karl—the priest in the family—delivered the eulogy. He, too, had known Grandma all his life and was able to share a wealth of information I had never even thought to seek out. He spoke of how her legacy would live on, both in her preserves and handicrafts, as well as through all of us. She had sponsored all of her siblings to follow her out of the Black Forest and to America. My grandfather stayed with her family when he was a soldier in World War I. When he returned to the states, he sent for her, a much younger woman. She traveled to Michigan by herself and married this for-

eigner. And she made it work. In short order, she arranged for her kin to follow her to the Midwest.

And while I knew my cousins, aunts, and uncles, I never knew the story behind them all until that sad day. And that felt awful. I could never again ask her a question about her childhood in Germany, how she felt about traveling abroad by herself, what she felt for my grandfather when she first met him. I couldn't hear her merry, heavily accented voice share her unique story with me.

Don't let this happen to you. Use me as *a cautionary tale,* pull out your video camera, and discover your family history. Ask about ancestors, the homeland, heirlooms, and anything that will add to the rich tapestry of your family's story. This could be the most rewarding, *connected* conversation you've ever had with your family.

What is your ethnic background?

notes

How did your family come to this country?

Do you speak any of your ancestral languages?

Do you like/miss any foods from your family's homeland?

If English is not your first language, do you still speak your native tongue? Do you dream in a different language?

Do you know any folktales or superstitions from your native country?

What is the most valuable thing you learned from your grandparents?

Did you know your great-grandparents at all? If so, what is your most vivid memory of them?

Was your grandmother known for any particular dish or recipe?

Do you feel connected to your ethnic background? In what way?

Have you ever visited your family's native country?

notes

Has anyone in your family studied your genealogy and started a family tree?

What is your most prized family heirloom?

Do you have any belongings from your parents or grandparents that you continue to use regularly?

Have you ever inherited anything?

Has anyone in your family tree ever made and lost a fortune?

Can your family be traced back to Ellis Island or another point of entry for immigrants?

Do you have any relatives who came to America from another country, or still live somewhere else? If so, do they have any customs, traditions, or beliefs that seem unique to their background?

Did your grandparents or parents face any opposition when getting married?

Are you aware of any tragedies that befell your ancestors?

What do you regret not being able to ask of a relative who passed away?

If given the opportunity to live in your family's homeland for a few years, would you do it? What would you hope to experience?

notes

What state or region did your family settle in? How did they end up there?

Describe your grandparents' house.

What was your grandparents' most prized possession?

Did your grandparents have any signature phrases, stories, or tricks?

Have you ever gone rummaging or antiquing with your grandparents or parents?

Do any relatives speak their native language, if other than English?

Are there any kids in the extended family who you think are ill-behaved?

In retrospect, would you have done anything differently as a parent?

Has anyone in the family experienced extreme poverty?

Who would be considered the black sheep in the family tree? Why?

notes

How would you label different members of the family (for instance, the Peter Pan, the ne'er-do-well, the workaholic)?

Growing up, who were you closest to in your family?

Did you ever wish you had more brothers and sisters? Fewer?

Do you ever wish you were born into a different family?

Why are you thankful that you were born into your particular family?

What has been the greatest lesson that you've learned from your family?

Are there any ancestors who you think you resemble?

Has there been any adoption in your family? Have you considered it?

Did you ever wonder if you were adopted?

If you were adopted through a closed process, have you ever wanted to track down your birth parents?

FAMILY HISTORY

If you were adopted, what sort of feelings do you have toward your birth parents? Your adopted parents?

What one word would sum up your family?

Is there anyone notable in your family lineage (politician, celebrity, royalty, pirate)?

Do you and your family share any genetic quirks?

What physical features do you hope live on in future generations?

What's the most disappointing family visit you've ever had?

Have you had to care for an elderly relative? Talk about the experience.

In their later years, did any of your relatives have regrets or insights that they wanted to share?

How did you cope with watching a parent or relative become more infirm in their later years?

Which relative do you think you are most like? Look like?

notes

FAMILY HISTORY

notes

Does your marriage bear any resemblance to that of your parents?

What family trait are you most proud of?

Are you named after any relatives?

Are you worried or excited that you may turn into your parents someday?

Has anyone in your family tree ever had a brush with greatness, or been witness to a historical event?

Do you know if anyone in your family ever knew someone famous? Was anyone in your family famous or infamous?

Did you ever meet a relative, only to be surprised by how similar you were to each other?

If you were to write a history of your family, what would be the most important events or moments to include?

What parts of your family history do you most wish be handed down to future generations?

follow-up and additional questions

chapter 4

Now What?
Creating a Living History Online

Now that you've asked the questions and maybe even videotaped or recorded your relatives, what do you do with the great anecdotes and stories? You share them, of course!

Even with relatives flung to the far corners of the world, families can stay closer than ever with social networking. I've been knee-deep in social media for some time now and am continually amazed at how online platforms can be used to connect and build a community. Businesses promote themselves through Facebook fan pages, entrepreneurs find their audience through compelling tweets on Twitter, and individuals use it all to reconnect with former classmates and stay in touch with their many friends.

But for some reason, people tend to overlook the possibilities of how social media can be used to reach out and touch family. And the possibilities, if not endless, are many. Sites like YouTube, Flickr, and MyFamily.com allow users to create free accounts and post video, photos, and information. Chats, groups, and fan pages in Yahoo!, MySpace, and Facebook allow you to converse easily with a large group of people. Creating a "twibe" of your family in Twitter allows you to track your family members thoughts and activities in real time.

And the great thing is that, in many cases, you can designate the pages and groups as public or keep them private, with access granted only to your family if you favor discretion. Why not take advantage of these terrific sites when connecting with your relatives?

This chapter will take you through all the various social media outlets that can be best used for your living history, describing the various up- and downsides of each, explaining how to set up accounts, post files, and grant access to your family. However, keep in mind that social media changes daily and applications and platforms could crop up at any time that could also be embraced for family communication. Be open.

And be engaged. With the easy-to-follow tools available at your fingertips (via a keyboard), you'll get your family chatting it up like never before. In short order, you'll have a family wiki with areas for video and audio clips, recipes, chats and forums (threads like "family fact or fiction?" or "reunion planning," for instance), locations and dates of seminal family events (*Ellis Island, 1921*: Susanna Miltz arrived from Germany with the intention of marrying Lyman Worick of Sodus, Michigan; *6144 Lett Road, Sodus, Michigan, 1977*: John Worick broke his arm jumping off the shed next to the house), recent family photos, Twitter updates on what people are doing, and the like.

Aside from the Web, gathering all this information allows you to assemble one-of-a-kind gifts for family. Consider creating a "highlight reel" each year of the best clips the family provided and send it out as a DVD to everyone for the holidays. More and more computers are equipped with software that allows you to edit these bits pretty easily and with minimal knowledge. Take advantage of modern technology to preserve your family's unique past and forge closer bonds with siblings, parents, aunts, uncles, cousins, and in-laws. Create your living history—right this minute.

SOCIAL MEDIA 101

Even if you're not wading through the tide of social networking, you've probably dipped your toe in it, or at least have heard about it. What is it, *exactly*? Social media is an organized means of publishing whereby individuals can communicate—through text, audio, or video—directly with people they know or the entire world without the content being filtered through an editor or publisher. In other words, it's a way to instantly connect with others—like your family, for instance—though various online channels. Does that make sense? In the past, writing and posting letters have been how folks kept in touch. Now e-mail is a key way folks keep conversations going, and social networking sites have become effective means of maintaining and developing relationships in real time.

Not convinced? Well, consider this. Tens of millions of people use a social networking site like Facebook or Twitter on a daily basis. Just think of all the ways you could keep up to date on your mom's activities or stay in touch with that brother who lives clear across the country. You don't have to be online every second of every day. Unless it's required for your job, it's probably a really bad idea. But if you were to create exclusive channels for your family to stay in

touch, you'll end up saving everyone time while keeping your relationships fresh. If you can broadcast big news in one central location, you can avoid having to repeat yourself in multiple phone calls or e-mails and you can open up a group conversation, which can be a hoot.

Most of these networking tools and hosting sites are absolutely free for basic memberships. After experimenting, sampling, and giving a few sites a go, you can pick the platform that best suits your family. As your and your family's participation grows, you can then entertain a premium membership that will help to create a more robust experience for you and your relatives. So let's check out a few of the networking sites to see what might best work for you and your kin.

THE HEAVY HITTERS

 Facebook

I love Facebook. In fact, I'm addicted to it. Over the past few years, Facebook has grown by leaps and bounds and, at the time

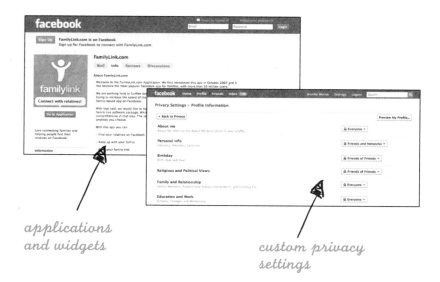

applications and widgets

custom privacy settings

of publication, has more than 300 million active users worldwide. Think about that.

But while it's big and wide reaching, you can still manage to make it small and intimate. It might not make sense to limit your "friends" to just family members but you *can* tag your kin with the FamilyLink.com application, as well as post updates, photos, and links to them only via a "family stream." It's a nice way to incorporate your family's conversation within the bigger platform of Facebook.

Specifically, Facebook is an efficient way to connect with family members who have already spent considerable time creating and maintaining a Facebook account. Rather than reinvent the wheel with another social networking platform, "friend" and tag your relatives already on Facebook and send invitations to the folks who haven't quite boarded the Facebook train. Once you've got your family circle on the site, consider posting questions on the "family stream" on a weekly basis. This will keep them engaged in the site and you.

Facebook is fully loaded with applications and widgets to link to other sites. News and aggregate sites, blogs, and other networking sites often have buttons you can click on to quickly post items to Facebook, making it a snap to share information. You can also post status updates and photos from many phones these days, so you can stay connected when you're on the go.

But beware, family members will be able to look at your wall and see all the comments you and your friends are making. If you would rather not clue in your parents or your nephew on your shenanigans, incriminating photographs (your friends may tag you without your permission), ribald sense of humor, or political beliefs, you'd best look for another social network to connect with family. You don't want to cause a slight scandal by ignoring a family member's friend request because you're afraid of what they might see. Personally, I decided that I didn't want to draw a distinction between what I say to friends and what I let my family see, so I let it all hang out there on Facebook. But every time I post a political clip that I know my family won't agree with, I pause for a moment. If this sounds like more trouble than it's worth, move on. There are plenty of other sites that will suit your needs beautifully.

Twitter

I'm obsessed with Twitter these days, I'm not going to lie. When I first heard about this micro-blogging site, I wondered why in the world I would ever want to post 140-character updates or comments to friends and strangers. At first blush, it seemed just plain weird. A few people started following me and I posted a few half-hearted updates.

Then Twitter started to work its magic on me. I started tweeting with earnest. Strangers would see my tweets (what the 140-character updates have come to be called) and respond, I got direct messages from folks looking to connect and, yes, sometimes sell something. Pretty quickly, you can distinguish between people you want to stay connected to and those who you want to kick to the cyber-curb. I've weeded out those social media whores ("smores") and now have a vibrant, active community of friends and strangers with whom I can chat, query when I need information, and promote my various writing.

But here's the thing: you have to be active on Twitter or it's probably better to stay off it altogether. Sure, you can have a media blackout when you're on vacation or slammed at work, but part of the unspoken code on Twitter—at least, in my opinion—is that you have to agree to be part of the conversation and the community. If not, people will notice and unfollow you.

How does this relate to family? Well, *140 characters has its limits,* that's obvious. You can post only about two sentences at a time. That said, you can do a surprisingly effective job of conversing and updating in such limited space. If you're excited about a trip to your hometown, you don't really need more than a sentence. If you want to share a funny video of your toddler, you need only to describe the clip and display a URL that links back to YouTube or another hosting site. You can set your Twitter account to private so that only your followers can see your tweets. If you don't set up your account this way, anyone searching for key words can see your tweets. Most people using Twitter opt for a public account, because they want their links to be viewed or their tweets to surface on searches (many use Twitter for branding, advertising, and promotion). For example, if I have a new blog post, I might post the following tweet: "A publishing insider discusses the future of traditional publishing: http://jenniferworick.blogspot .com." I want as many people to see this as possible so it doesn't make sense to restrict my tweets. However, if you want to post more personal items to just friends and family, such as "Molly's birthday party was off the hook; check out the

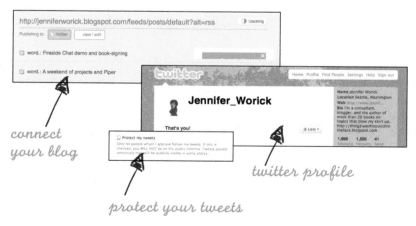

connect your blog

protect your tweets

twitter profile

Beyond the Family Tree

highlights at www.youtube.com/abcdefg12345," it makes sense to limit viewing of your updates and profile to your inner circle. Just go to your account settings and click on the box next to "Protect my tweets." You can also set up a separate Twitter account that you dedicate to family updates only.

If you have a blog or another platform for family videos and information, consider inviting your family to set up Twitter profiles so you can alert them when you post new content to your site. No matter the number of followers you have, Twitter is an excellent way to broadcast news to a group. You can send tweets from many different mobile phones so you can stay connected even if you're away from your computer.

While Twitter is wildly popular with good reason, there are potential drawbacks. There is the possibility that you'll become *too* connected to certain family members. Aunt Nan might really take to tweeting . . . every fifteen minutes, which can clutter up your Twitter stream with a whole lot of useless information (or political views that you don't really want to hear). If folks are just getting under way with it, you may want to consider sending out a few guidelines for use so they don't start tweeting the mundane. No one really needs to know that Aunt Nan just read the newspaper or reorganized her sweaters. On the other hand, some relatives might be reluctant to post with any frequency, thinking the whole world can see their tweets or that they don't have anything interesting to report. You can set the tone by sending out a lot of lively, engaging tweets at the start. Ask questions that invite responses from family members. Once you guide them through some initial tweeting, the family should be up and running with a high comfort level. And it's easy, using applications like Twitterfeed, to create automatic links between Twitter and other platforms so every time you post to your blog, it automatically creates a new tweet. You can adjust your settings within various networking sites so that new tweets automatically get forwarded to another site (such as Facebook) and update your status. It may seem daunting at first but once it's all set up, you can just enjoy the ease of technology.

YouTube

I suspect you've watched at least one video of a cat on a keyboard or a guy shaking his way through the evolution of dance. Admit it. It's okay; you're not alone. YouTube is a wildly popular site for posting video.

At first blush, it might just seem like a place to *watch* stuff. But the comment component under each video often yields a conversation centered around the video. YouTube is easy to use, with a large amount of storage space and easy step-by-step instructions to upload video. While most people chose to post video for the world to hopefully see, you can mark your account or videos as private, so only your family has viewing privileges. Mom *really* might not like that vacation

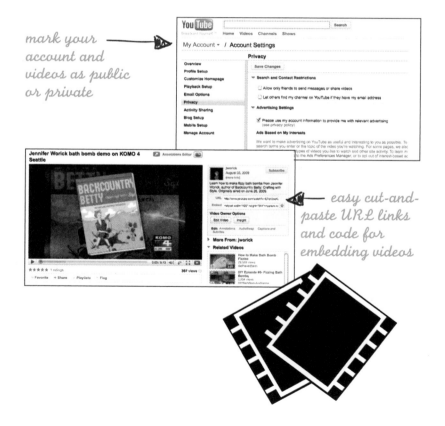

mark your account and videos as public or private

easy cut-and-paste URL links and code for embedding videos

footage of her in a bathing suit on display to strangers.

YouTube does have some limitations. It does what it does very well, and that's focus on hosting digital video content. But it's not the most robust forum for written discussion: you really can only comment on a video; it's not intended to start separate conversations or forums. Aside from the videos you upload, there are not a lot of other features to keep your family engaged on the site (aside from the millions of videos that aren't related to you). In addition, because of its focus, its video-dependent discourse requires everyone to possess camcorders or webcams, as well as the know-how to create and upload digital video.

While you may not find YouTube the best platform for all of your family's networking needs, think about using it to host your video. YouTube provides easy cut-and-paste code, in case you want to link to or embed a video on a blog or elsewhere on the Web.

Flickr

Flickr is to photography what YouTube is to video content. It allows you to upload tons of digital photos (and now video as well), organize them into groups, tag them with labels and names, and then share them. Viewers can leave comments under any photo, and a community of your contacts can be built up around photography.

I've used Flickr to post arty shots as well as photos of events, be it photos of road signs or pictures from my best friend's bridal shower.

It's a snap to create a profile for yourself and, if privacy's important to you, there are loads of settings you can turn on to *protect your account*. When you set up an account, you can invite family members to join or, if they are already active on Flickr, to become a contact. In the settings, you can tag contacts and differentiate between friends and family members for additional organization. When posting photos to Flickr, you can allow anyone to see it or limit viewing to "friends" or "family" (meaning you can keep your friends away from your baby photos, and Grandma away from those incriminating keg stand shots). You can also hide your images and profile from public searches, allowing only your approved contacts to see you and your work. While it may seem

simple set up, free basic account

easy upload for photos and short video

quick links make it easy to add your photo to a set, post to a blog or wiki, e-mail, and more

that you're posting stuff on the Internet for the world to see, you can house your digital photography online and limit viewing to only the people you want to see it, in this case, your family.

When you post a photo, you or others can easily send it to a group, add it to a set of photos, post it to a blog (which is a great feature if you have a family blog or wiki to which you'd like to add a photo), or e-mail to someone. All those features are available through buttons above or next to a photo, which makes Flickr a good way to house photos, even if you want to post them elsewhere as well.

With a free account, Flickr allows you to upload up to 100MB of new photos *and* video every month, which should be ample if you are just getting under way. Video clips have to be no longer than 90 seconds and no larger than 150MB. You can't upload more than two videos per month. If you plan on posting video regularly, you will need to upgrade to a Pro account (which runs $25 a year) or choose another platform (such as YouTube) to host your footage.

What does all this mean for your family? Well, if your relatives have lots of photos that they'd like to share with one another, Flickr or another photo-hosting site is an obvious platform to use. If digital photography is the primary way you plan to communicate, create a Flickr account. It's a fun and easy way to keep in touch through visuals. You can let folks know that, when new images are up, they can comment on them. However, while Flickr is a well-designed, function-al, and user-friendly site, it has a pretty specific use. As your need or desire to add other elements to the conversation grows, you may find Flickr too limited for your purposes. If down the road you get a camcorder, you'll be disappointed with your basic account because you won't be able to post much footage. If you want to start sharing recipes among your family, it will be tricky to create a library of dishes with photography-centric platform. Planning a family reunion? It's best to look elsewhere for an information-sharing site.

MySpace

Remember a few short years ago when MySpace was all the rage? Everyone was quick to update their status lines and post information to the bulletin board on their page. People sent messages back and forth to each other; some even live chatted. Users customized their pages with colorful or artistic backgrounds. But then Facebook was opened up to the public and My Space became marginalized as people flocked to the other social network. Sure, folks still use MySpace but it seems to have become the bastion of bands, recording artists, and reality-show castoffs. It's unfortunate, because people have spent significant time building their pages and developing a community. And it's a very functional and robust platform for reaching out to your family.

MySpace has millions of users everyday, and its functionality is more than adequate for you and your family. Much like Facebook, you can set up a personal profile, load it up with all sorts of information, link a blog to it, and e-mail and instant message with your friends (i.e., family members who also join and connect with you). You can protect your account so that only your friends can see your page. You can post photos or upload video that your family can comment on, and you can write a blog directly on MySpace or link to one. You could easily host a family blog on the site. You can create a group for your family, where you and others can broadcast news about relatives or gatherings, and post topics for discussion. You can easily change your status and mood so family can stay connected to you and your thoughts on a daily basis. A bar along the bottom of your screen will alert you when friends are online and available to instant

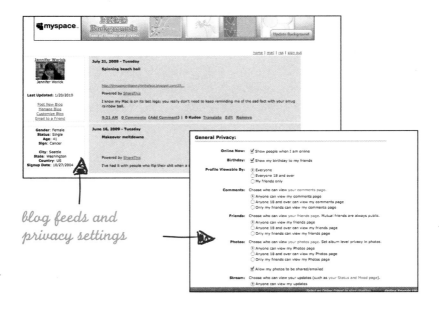

blog feeds and
privacy settings

message so you can chat informally and immediately with family and stay up to date with someone's daily triumphs and challenges.

If you've got a good number of family members already up and running on MySpace, this might be a good choice for connecting with family. However, be advised that Facebook has eclipsed MySpace in popularity and the lack of variable privacy settings allow other friends to mix with family, so if you have other friends aside from family, there's no way to bar them from information you just intend for your relatives' eyes.

Yahoo! Groups

You probably have used Yahoo!'s phenomenal search engine more than once. But did you know about all the other great features that Yahoo! offers? If you look on Yahoo!'s home page, you'll see that you can access e-mail (by creating a free Yahoo! account), live chats, news, games, and a whole passel of other things. And if you notice, you can create and join groups. You can specify it as a family group and name it something as simple as worickfamily@ yahoogroups.com. You can set up

a group within minutes and then you can get busy using it as a hub for family activity.

The first order of business is inviting family members to join. After they register (they might have a Yahoo! account already, since it's such a popular portal), they'll have access to all sorts of tools. When you send out an e-mail, it goes out to everyone in the group. You can post messages, upload files and photos, link to other sites, keep a family calendar, and even create a database of names, numbers, and vital information (such as birthdays). In particular, you can create polls, which would be a fun way of seeing what family members think on subjects both serious and silly. And like most other platforms, you can easily *restrict membership* to just those whom you invite and have different levels of privacy on the material posted within the

set up/monitor private groups

group. All in all, creating a Yahoo! group is an easy-peasy way of staying connected.

However, there are a few limitations of using a Yahoo! group as your primary way to connect with the whole family. Anyone can see the messages posted on the group's front page (although other elements, such as photos, can be designated private and accessed by the group only).

MyFamily.com

This is the Cadillac of social media sites designed exclusively for families. A basic membership is free and the site is loaded with every possible feature you'd want to use to connect with your family. Go there now and poke around. On the home page, you'll be able to click a link and take a tour through the site's features, which include groups, photos, video, discussions, family tree, and a calendar.

I can't say enough good things about this site. You can create different groups for different branches on your family tree (your mother's side of the family as opposed to your dad's side, for example). It has all the robustness of Facebook or MySpace but you can limit participation to your family only. Once you set up an account, you can create a profile, start discussion topics, or begin a family tree that others can help to fill in. You can upload photos and group them into albums, post videos, and list events and even your travel schedule. I once found out that my stepbrother and I were both in London at the same time . . . after the fact. *Don't let this happen to you;* broadcasting your schedule can help far-flung family members figure out how they can cross paths with you.

But first things first: invite your family. Get them started with just a profile and then send them regular e-mails to encourage their participation.

If you don't have a lot of family members already invested in Facebook or another popular site, this is a great place to land. And no matter what each relative's strength is, they'll find something to embrace on the site. Love to write? They can type away in the discussion section or upload files. The family genealogist can get to work on the digital family tree. Photographers and videographers can post images and video to their heart's content for others to "ooh" and "aah" and comment on. The cooks in the family can upload recipes, with photos if they like. The analytical relative who loves his spreadsheet can organize the calendar for the family. And everyone can have a good time creating a profile for the rest of the folks to check out. If you're an obsessive Twitter user, you can update your status as often as you want (like Twitter, you get 140 characters to let people know what's on your mind). If you have an eye for design, you can dress up your family's pages with interesting backgrounds (there are more options if you upgrade your membership).

I don't know if it's good or bad, but the site also offers a stream of merchandise that you can purchase as keepsakes or gifts. However, it's easy to bypass this feature and log in to your profile directly. With an upgraded membership, MyFamily.com assigns you a URL so your family can easily access its group. And as with other sites, you can choose different levels of privacy depending on whether you want people to find your group during searches.

The upgraded membership costs $2.50 a month and gives members ten times the memory for uploading content. This enhanced membership allows you to create and design themes, it gives you a personalized URL, and it is ad-free. Once you find that your family is using this site with gusto, it might

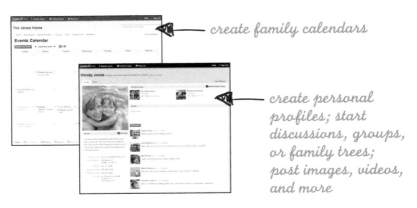

create family calendars

create personal profiles; start discussions, groups, or family trees; post images, videos, and more

make sense to chip in for the nominal upgrade fee. After chapters 1 and 2, you're going to have a lot of great video to post!

 Cozi.com

Like MyFamily.com, Cozi.com is a site designed specifically for families. While I suspect young families living under one roof are the primary users of the site, you can co-opt some of its features for your extended family's purposes. While you might not need to use the "to-do list" function, you can use the family journal like a shared blog or website, inviting select relatives to read the blog. You can even send e-mail alerts when there is new content posted. In addition, Cozi has a shopping list feature, which I think could be used for Christmas wish lists rather than that monthly trek to Costco. There's a color-coded family calendar where relatives can post birthdays, reunions, and even their travel schedules. While it's not technically designed for far-flung families and isn't as robust as some other free sites, you can tailor it to your family's needs and use it to keep in touch and keep relationships fresh and up to the moment.

OTHER RESOURCES

Blogs

There are all sorts of statistics flying around about the number of blogs (short for Web logs) that have been started (tens of millions), the number of blogs that are active (again, tens of millions), and how many are started per second (nine). But these numbers are constantly changing so it's hard to rattle off any statistics with any accuracy. But what I'm 100 percent sure about is that blogs are here to stay and they are an excellent source of information and entertainment.

You've probably read a few blogs, even if you don't write or contribute to one. Individuals and businesses use them in all sorts of creative and strategic ways. They can serve as an online diary, a magazine, a news source, and a branding tool.

I've been blogging for a few years now and currently maintain two with frequent posts. One is a humor blog and the other covers my personal and professional musings. And I've found them both to be excellent ways of reaching out and connecting with an audience. Sometimes that audience is my family.

Blogs are an important component to social networking. While they can certainly be one-way communications, increasingly they are becoming a fun way to *organize conversations around a topic.* And blogs can have multiple authors, which could make them an ideal platform for your family, if y'all like to write. Popular blog sites like Blogger and Wordpress are free and easily customizable. You can pick an existing template as your design, choose a color palette, assign blog authors (if you choose to have multiple contributors), and get up and running in no time.

Wordpress is being constantly developed by a large community of bloggers and Web professionals. In its basic form, it's designed as an easy-to-use and excellent blogging platform with the ability to become much more. When first setting up a blog, Wordpress will walk you through the initial configuration and settings so you can get going while you're learning the ropes and acquiring advanced knowledge. Through open source

(which means that its code is accessible to the public), Wordpress is available to install on your own server if you want to host your blog yourself. If you think that you might evolve your blog into a full-blown, robust site, Wordpress with its extensible nature is a good choice for a blogging platform. Typepad is another popular blogging platform (featuring benefits similar to Wordpress) with a downloadable version called Moveable Type. The platform is well supported, has a large community, and is frequently updated with new features.

Another option is Blogger, the platform I have long used. I have quite enjoyed the ease of it; like Wordpress, it's a snap to get started (I think it took me about an hour to set up and design my first blog). Blogger will walk you through the initial steps and does a good job of explaining the various settings (privacy, comment moderation, RSS feeds, number of posts shown on landing page, etc.). I've found it rather easy to embed sharing widgets so that people can easily send my posts around the Web. Linking to YouTube has been a bit spotty and sometimes the code for embedding video results in awkward

pre-existing blog templates

DIY blogging software

allow multiple users for one blog

placement that doesn't quite fit into the template properly. The templates are somewhat limited so you can usually spot a Blogger account a mile away. But they are clean and attractive so I don't find that a problem for me. It's also easy for multiple users to author a blog. I'd suggest poking around on a few Blogger blogs and seeing how other users have made the templates their own.

If you want to create a single- or multiple-author blog centered around your family, I'd suggest writing a few posts and then sending e-mails to your family, inviting them to comment on posts or participate. They can either send you items to post or you can give them access and a tutorial to allow them to join in the blogging fun. But make sure they are committed to participation; otherwise you'll be shouldering the blogging duties and writing about your life and no one else's. This is fine and dandy, but not necessarily a well-rounded family blog with lots of information and content coming in from various fronts.

Wikis

Like blogs, you've probably eyeballed a wiki or two. Basically, a wiki (the Hawaiian word for "fast") is a Web site that uses software to allow for easy creation and editing of multiple pages. The markup language is easy, allowing multiple users to contribute to the site. Wikis are most often used this way, as collaborative websites, Wikipedia being the most well known of them. Multiple users can contribute content to them simply by registering. If something is posted that the moderator (usually the person who created the wiki site) or the other users don't like, it can be removed in short order.

Sounds great, right? Well, wikis *are* great, and particularly suited to our purposes of family communication. Free services, such as Wetpaint, allow you to create a wiki for free. Wetpaint's wiki community is quite active, and the most popular wikis have been set up as fan sites for television shows. This makes a lot of sense, if you think about it. After a compelling or controversial episode, viewers want to dissect, talk, rave, and complain about it. And often, there are only a few other friends and family who share your enthusiasm. So you look online for a community. Twitter is fine for real-time conversations but there are a lot of other nontopic tweets clogging up the feed. So why not head to a site dedicated to your show? In addition to discussion forums, there are photos, video, updates, and news about your fa-

vorite show. It's like the mother ship is calling you home.

So how can you use a wiki to stay connected with your family? Much like MyFamily.com, you can create a robust site around which your family can cyber-congregate. Unlike Facebook, you don't have to be a member of a larger group to set up a family site. It can be private or open for the whole world to see. You can add pages for recipes, stories, photo galleries (worst school photo, for example), video, etc. There are all sorts of widgets you can embed in your wiki. For example, you can add a chat widget so you can instant message with any relatives via the wiki. You can use the messaging tool to send notes to everyone on your site; they'll receive them via the e-mail they used to register on the wiki. Or you can add a voting feature and take a poll of who's the most thoughtful grandchild, where to host the next reunion, or the worst family roadtrip. You can bring sincerity or humor to the site as you and your family see fit. Either way, you're sure to start and continue the conversation if you have engaging features that involve relatives in some way and encourage them to open up.

Wikis, like many of the other platforms, are an ideal way to plan family reunions, posting information and changes in real time. You can efficiently post and update all sorts of lists on a wiki, including birthdays, holiday wish lists, wedding registries, and family numbers and addresses. Whatever would get sent out via mail, e-mail, or phone, consider posting to the wiki and saving yourself and your family massive amounts of time.

There are just a few easy steps to create a basic wiki and from there, the point person can add further bells and whistles to the site. Once you've set it up, you can create new pages or sections, perhaps designing pages for different segments of the family. For instance, there are already your mother's and father's sides of the family. Add to that stepfamilies and spouse's kin and you could easily have six different pages for various families within the larger family tree.

 Skype

While Skype isn't the ideal medium for staying connected with your family as a whole, I need to mention it because it's a handy tool for talking with far-flung family. It is a software application that allows you to

free online calls or video chats with various privacy levels

make free online calls to one or several people. I've enjoyed conference calls with friends all over the country, even video chats with my brother when he was stationed in Kuwait. While Skype isn't suitable for creating an online gathering place, it is an ancillary means of communicating.

THE ONGOING ONLINE EXPERIENCE

So how do you use these many great social networks to your best advantage? Once you choose a site or platform to connect with your family and get going, reach out. Gather e-mails from relatives and send out invites to close and distant relatives. Ask your close relatives to expand the search and put out the call for participants. Ring up the computer-challenged ones and talk them through the process of using the Internet. This might take some doing. When my mother first discovered the "interweb," it was as if she had suddenly materialized out of the Middle Ages. She didn't understand any of the language that I take for granted. I had to explain terms like "cursor" and "mouse." So I learned to be patient and go slow. Show your relative just what they need to know to get to the family site. Write down instructions so they have something to refer to when you're not there. Be prepared to field a few panicked calls.

Once you get everyone online and directed toward a social network, a few things could happen. Folks could start contributing with gusto, checking in regularly, and posting items. Or all of your relatives could rely on you to keep it going and not add anything to the conversation. Most likely, it will be somewhere in between. Family members will check in periodically when they have time and might post photos after a birthday party

or send out their Christmas letter online. Chances are, you'll need to prod them along. Work on keeping the conversation fresh. Even if you don't have compelling video to post or anything new to report, you can keep the dialogue lively. Ask one of the provocative questions from chapter 3. Create a poll. Post a childhood photo. Update others on your summer vacation plans. Get in the habit of interacting with the site weekly and hopefully others will follow suit.

Whatever you create online for your family to gather around, be assured that it is just the tip of the iceberg. A little hunting and pecking around the Internet will reveal a host of other secure and viable options for you and your family to explore. Just remember to keep your purpose in mind. If it's unlikely that the majority of family members will post photos or video clips, stick to a site that can organize and store a lot of text. Create a discussion forum with different threads, instead. Play to your relatives' strengths and encourage participation at every turn. In short order, you'll have a vibrant dialogue among all of your family members, no matter their age or geographic location.

Conclusion:
Continuing the Conversation

Talking with family can be hard. But with a few strategies, a bit of equipment, and whole arsenal of interesting questions, creating meaningful experiences and conversations can become the norm and not the exception. It's so easy to tune out around challenging relatives and tune in to your own running monologue. Oh, you are probably justified in it, but chances are that you won't have a good time and your time spent with family will quickly become a missed opportunity. More and more, we find ourselves flung far and wide and once-close relatives drift apart, gathering for only holidays and big events.

What happens in the meantime is up to you. Carve time out of your busy schedule to talk, *really* talk, with your family members. Whether or not the camera is turned on, suss out rich memories and stories and you'll find ways to connect, to feel close. If nothing else, you'll be humored or moved.

And once you've opened new lines of communication, resist the tendency to put everything on cruise control and sit back. *Don't!* This is a fantastic opportunity to go further. Track down distant relatives; get the rest of your family as involved as possible. Continue to ask questions, even in regular phone calls or e-mails. Once you've learned about each other's personal history, ask about their current hopes, dreams, and frustrations. The beauty of relationships is that there's no limit to how close or intimate you can become. Use *Beyond the Family Tree* as a launchpad toward dynamic and ever-evolving family relations. Thanksgiving conversations and weekly phone calls will never be the same!

Appendix

Feel free to photocopy this log or write directly on these pages to keep track of the relatives you are interviewing. If there's more information you want to capture, or you have a large number of relatives to interview, consider creating your own spreadsheet, using this log as a guide.

Name: **Dad's Name Here**

Relation to you: **Father**

Phone number: **718-233-4455**

E-mail: **dadsemail@home.com**

Contacted? **Yes 5-12-10**

Interview scheduled? **6-22-10**

Interview completed? **Yes**

Interview location: **Parents' house**

Interviewer: **Mary Lee Springer (Daughter)**

Format (circle) (video) (audio) *written (other)* **photos**

Uploaded to Web? **Facebook, Flickr, MyFamily.com**

PLACE PHOTO HERE

Name:

Relation to you:

Phone number:

E-mail:

Contacted?

Interview scheduled?

Interview completed?

Interview location:

Interviewer:

Format (circle) video audio written (other)

Uploaded to Web?

PLACE PHOTO HERE

Name:

Relation to you:

Phone number:

E-mail:

Contacted?

Interview scheduled?

Interview completed?

Interview location:

Interviewer:

Format (circle) video audio written (other)

Uploaded to Web?

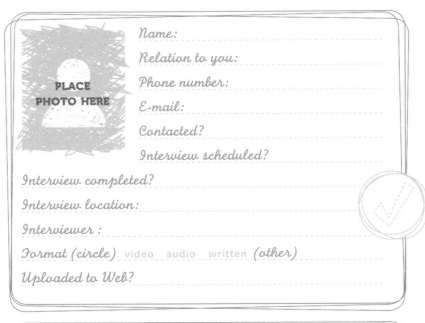

Name:

Relation to you:

Phone number:

E-mail:

Contacted?

Interview scheduled?

Interview completed?

Interview location:

Interviewer :

Format (circle) video audio written (other)

Uploaded to Web?

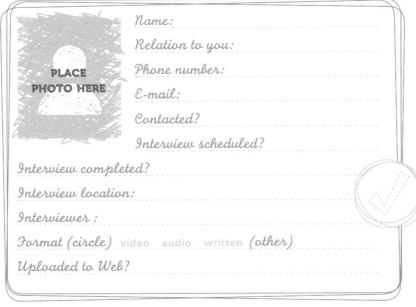

Name:

Relation to you:

Phone number:

E-mail:

Contacted?

Interview scheduled?

Interview completed?

Interview location:

Interviewer :

Format (circle) video audio written (other)

Uploaded to Web?

Beyond the Family Tree

PLACE PHOTO HERE

Name:

Relation to you:

Phone number:

E-mail:

Contacted?

Interview scheduled?

Interview completed?

Interview location:

Interviewer :

Format (circle) video   audio   written   (other)

Uploaded to Web?

PLACE PHOTO HERE

Name:

Relation to you:

Phone number:

E-mail:

Contacted?

Interview scheduled?

Interview completed?

Interview location:

Interviewer :

Format (circle) video   audio   written   (other)

Uploaded to Web?

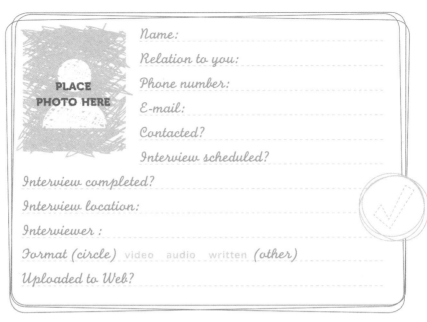

Beyond the Family Tree

Name:

Relation to you:

Phone number:

E-mail:

Contacted?

Interview scheduled?

Interview completed?

Interview location:

Interviewer :

Format (circle) video audio written *(other)*

Uploaded to Web?

Name:

Relation to you:

Phone number:

E-mail:

Contacted?

Interview scheduled?

Interview completed?

Interview location:

Interviewer :

Format (circle) video audio written *(other)*

Uploaded to Web?

MY FAMILY TREE

Use this chart as a springboard to chronicling your roots. As you learn more about your extended family and ancestors, you may want to create a chart or use one of the online tools to record names as well as birth, death, and marriage dates.

Me
spouse
children

Father
siblings

niece/nephews

Sibling
spouse
children

Sibling
spouse
children

Mother
siblings

niece/nephews

Sibling
spouse
children

Grandfather

siblings

niece/nephews

Great-grandfather

Great-grandmother

Grandmother

siblings

niece/nephews

Great-grandfather

Great-grandmother

Grandfather

siblings

niece/nephews

Great-grandfather

Great-grandmother

Grandmother

siblings

niece/nephews

Great-grandfather

Great-grandmother

COVERING THE BASES

There is a lot of information to cover, so use this list to help organize family conversations around topics. You'll get a wider variety of anecdotes, and you can tailor interviews to each relative's interest and personal history.

Relationships
Relatives to talk with on this topic:

_____

_____

_____

_____

_____

Youth
Relatives to talk with on this topic:

_____

_____

_____

_____

_____

Education and Career
Relatives to talk with on this topic:

_____

_____

_____

_____

_____

Pop Culture and the Arts

Relatives to talk with on this topic:

_____

_____

_____

_____

Food and Drink

Relatives to talk with on this topic:

_____

_____

_____

_____

Holidays and Special Occasions

Relatives to talk with on this topic:

_____

_____

_____

_____

Health and the Body

Relatives to talk with on this topic:

_____

_____

_____

_____

Faith
Relatives to talk with on this topic:

Home and Travel
Relatives to talk with on this topic:

Politics, Law, and Country
Relatives to talk with on this topic:

Leisure Pursuits
Relatives to talk with on this topic:

Hopes, Dreams, and Deep Thoughts
Relatives to talk with on this topic:

_____

_____

_____

_____

Family History
Relatives to talk with on this topic:

_____

_____

_____

_____

_____

INTERVIEW NOTES

Photocopy this form and use it to jot down notes and thoughts during conversations.

Relative:

Relation to you:

Birth date:

Date of interview:

Interviewer:

Location:

Format:

Equipment used:

Goals for interview:

Sensitive areas of questioning:

Known interests:

Key questions:

1.
2.
3.
4.
5.
6.
7.
8.
9.
10.

Follow-up questions:

1.
2.
3.
4.
5.
6.
7.
8.
9.
10.

interview notes

interview notes

ONLINE RESOURCES

Social networks

Facebook
facebook.com
Number-one social networking site where individuals can create profiles, link to their blogs, create fan or group pages, post status updates and notes, upload photos and video, and instant message with other members

Twitter
twitter.com
Microblogging site where members can post status updates no longer than 140 characters

YouTube
youtube.com
Popular social network where members can post and share video

Flickr
flickr.com
Popular social network where members can post and share photos

MySpace
myspace.com
Robust social networking site where individuals can set up profiles, link to their blogs, post status updates and bulletin items, upload photos and video, and instant message with other members

Yahoo! Groups
yahoogroups.com
A popular search engine that has many features, including the ability to create groups where members can post and share information with each other via a private or public account

MyFamily
myfamily.com
Social network designed specifically for families. Like Facebook or MySpace, members (after being approved by the family group) can set up profiles, post status updates, links, and bulletin items, upload photos and video, and

e-mail each other. In addition, families can create shared calendars of events, plan reunions, post recipes, and the like

Cozi
cozi.com
Much like MyFamily, Cozi allows you to create color-coded family calendars, lists, and a family journal. While its primary focus is for families living under one roof, you could customize this free site for your own family's needs

Blogging platforms and wikis

Wordpress
wordpress.com
Open-source blogging platform that allows users to, in short order, design a blog that one or several people can contribute to. Wordpress users are constantly developing new apps and widgets that allow users to truly customize a blog so that it can actually serve as a Web site

Blogger
blogger.com
Blogging platform that will guide users through setting up a blog in less than an hour using its design features, templates, and settings

Typepad
typepad.com
Like both Blogger and Wordpress, Typepad is a well-supported platform that allows users to set up a free account and design a blog using existing settings and templates

Wet Paint
wetpaint.com
Free platform that allows you to create a wiki that all family members can contribute to. You can post links, create calendars, develop pages for Christmas lists, address books, and birthdays, and upload photos and video

Skype
skype.com
Download Skype's software and call anyone in the world for free through your computer. If your computer is equipped with a webcam (you can purchase inexpensive external webcams as well), you can see relatives while talking with them. Skype is also a great tool for conducting conference calls when people are scattered around the country

Jennifer Worick is the author or coauthor of more than twenty books, including *Simple Gifts*, *The Prairie Girl's Guide to Life*, and the *New York Times* bestseller, *The Worst-Case Scenario Survival Handbook: Dating and Sex*. In addition, she is a lecturer, blogger, freelance writer, social media consultant, and all-around crafty girl. Originally from southwestern Michigan, she now lives in Seattle and remains close with her family, figuratively if not geographically, through lively conversations via social networks, Skype, e-mail, blogs, and good old-fashioned phone calls, letters, and visits. You can find her at jenniferworick.com.